MEETING AND KNOWING

Acts 1:8

REV. ERNEST ADDO

Unless otherwise stated, all Scripture quotations are taken from the *King James Version* of the Bible.
All Greek and Hebrew word definitions given are taken from *The Strongest Strong's Exhaustive Concordance of the Bible.*

Published 2016 by Little Books Publications, United Kingdom

First Printing 2016

Email Ernest Addo:

ernest.addo1@yahoo.com

Find out more about Ernest Addo at:

www.facebook.com/LivingJesusTabernacle

ISBN: 978-0-9932250-3-1

Printed by College Hill Press

DEDICATION

I dedicate this book to my wonderful friend,
The Blessed Holy Spirit.

CONTENTS

PREFACE

Our Christian life begins with the Holy Spirit. The conviction of the Holy Spirit marks the starting point of our born again journey. Yet many believers do not have a relationship with the Holy Spirit. What is even more tragic is that many do not even know Him, let alone to have a relationship with Him. I have seen Christians literally run out of church services when the Holy Spirit was moving because they thought it was the devil moving in the congregation.

This is very sad because if a Christian does not have a relationship with the blessed Holy Spirit, it means that Christian is lost and is still walking in darkness. No wonder there are so many 'alleged' Christians in our churches today. True transformation of a Christian's life is as a result of the Holy Spirit's activities in the Christian's life.

Apostle Paul encountered this problem when he met the believers at Ephesus. He asked them whether they had received the Holy Ghost since they received Jesus Christ into their lives. The answer they gave was very shocking. They said to Paul that they had not even heard of any Holy Ghost.

And it came to pass, that, while Apollos was at Corinth, Paul having passed through the upper coasts came to Ephesus: and finding certain disciples,

He said unto them, Have ye received the Holy Ghost since ye believed? And they said unto him, We have not so much as heard whether there be any Holy Ghost.

Acts 19:1-2

We must realise that any church without the Holy Spirit is not a church and so it is with any Christian who does not have a relationship with the Holy Spirit. The Christian walk is a supernatural walk and the Holy Spirit is the one who has been given to us by the Lord to help us with this walk.

I am writing this book to introduce the Holy Spirit to every Christian in the body of Christ. I pray that by the time you finish reading, you will have a personal relationship with the Holy Spirit and begin to experience the mighty presence of God. He is longing to draw you closer to Himself. He is near to all those who are hungry to know Him.

Blessed are they which do hunger and thirst after righteousness: for they shall be filled.

Matthew 5:6

Chapter 1

MY ENCOUNTER WITH THE HOLY SPIRIT

When I became born again, I read a book called Good Morning Holy Spirit by Pastor Benny Hinn. As a newly born again Christian, I did not know much about the Holy Spirit and just like the disciples at Ephesus, I had no relationship with Him. But as I read how Pastor Benny encountered the Holy Spirit and how the Holy Spirit transformed his life, I was filled with the desire and hunger to know Him. There is a particular scripture in Good Morning Holy Spirit that became very meaningful to me as I read the book.

For ye have not received the spirit of bondage again to fear; but ye have received the Spirit of adoption, whereby we cry, Abba, Father.

Romans 8:15

I began to use this scripture in Romans 8:15 to pray. Little did I know that I was about to encounter the Holy Spirit. I had seen how in everyday life people adopt children and take them as their own. They train them, feed them, clothe them, take them to school and want the best for them. So I said to myself that, if human beings are capable of doing this, then according to Romans 8:15 the Holy Spirit can also adopt me. You see, at salvation, the Holy Spirit indwells in every believer. But we cannot stop there, we must know Him personally. So I prayed without ceasing, asking the Holy Spirit to adopt me and make me His child, to educate me and train me in the Lord.

One day, while I was in a church service at the University campus, I had a dramatic encounter with the Holy Spirit. Suddenly, the Holy Spirit came upon me and I was overshadowed with the power of God. I began to shake uncontrollably on the floor. I had never experienced something like that before but there I was lying on the floor with the power of God all over me. It was such a sweet presence that you do not want to let go. Following that experience, hands were laid on me and I received the baptism of the Holy Spirit with the evidence of speaking in tongues. After this encounter, my Christian life changed. I was now able to pray for long hours and understand the word of God. I also began to have dreams and visions. The Lord started to show me my future through dreams and visions. I saw myself several times ministering on stage with such a strong presence of God that many people were on the floor having fallen under the power of the Holy Spirit. I saw myself walking into hospitals to pray for the sick and to raise the dead. I was constantly experiencing His mighty presence and power.

My friend, the dreams and the visions the Lord showed me are happening even now. I am now a full-time minister of the Gospel of Jesus Christ, preaching, teaching and healing with signs and wonders following. The Lord answered my prayer by allowing the Holy Spirit to adopt me. He is my dearest friend and companion and He is still teaching me the word of God and providing guidance for my life and ministry.

I urge you to pray to also encounter Him. He will change and transform your life if you draw closer to Him. He will open your eyes to the truth of God's word. He will open your eyes to the spiritual realm through dreams and visions. He will transform your whole life and being to become a great person and a mighty instrument for God.

Dear Holy Spirit, I want to know You.
I am longing and yearning to meet You.
Please draw me closer to Yourself.
Please adopt me, train me and bring me up in the fear of the Lord.
In Jesus name, Amen.

Chapter 2

THE HOLY SPIRIT AND THE GODHEAD

The Godhead is made up of God the Father, God the Son and God the Holy Spirit. These three are one and equal. Christianity does not teach that we have three gods but one God.

Hear, O Israel: The LORD our God is one LORD.

Deuteronomy 6:4

Thus saith the Lord the King of Israel, and his redeemer the Lord of hosts; I am the first, and I am the last; and beside me there is no God.

Isaiah 44:6

And Jesus answered him, The first of all the commandments is, Hear, O Israel; The Lord our God is one Lord:

Mark 12:29

But to us there is but one God, the Father, of whom are all things, and we in him; and one Lord Jesus Christ, by whom are all things, and we by him.

1 Corinthians 8:6

Now a mediator is not a mediator of one, but God is one.

Galatians 3:20

The Holy Spirit is the Spirit of God as the scriptures tell us in Romans 15:19 and 2 Corinthians 3:3.

Through mighty signs and wonders, by the power of the Spirit of God; so that from Jerusalem, and round about unto Illyricum, I have fully preached the gospel of Christ.

Romans 15:19

Forasmuch as ye are manifestly declared to be the epistle of Christ ministered by us, written not with ink, but with the Spirit of the living God; not in tables of stone, but in fleshy tables of the heart.

2 Corinthians 3:3

The Holy Spirit is also referred to as the Spirit of Jesus Christ in Philippians 1:19, Galatians 4:6 and 1 Peter 1:11.

For I know that this shall turn to my salvation through your prayer, and the supply of the Spirit of Jesus Christ.

Philippians 1:19

And because ye are sons, God hath sent forth the Spirit of his Son into your hearts, crying, Abba, Father.

Galatians 4:6

Searching what, or what manner of time the Spirit of Christ which was in them did signify, when it testified beforehand the sufferings of Christ, and the glory that should follow.

1 Peter 1:11

Some think of the Holy Spirit as being lesser than God the Father and God the Son but this is not so. The Holy Spirit is also God Himself. John 4:24 tells us that God is a Spirit.

God is a Spirit: and they that worship him must worship him in spirit and in truth.

John 4:24

Furthermore, in 2 Corinthians 3:17, the word of God clearly states that *"now the Lord is that Spirit and where the Spirit of the Lord is there is liberty."* In 1 Corinthians 15:45, we see that the first Adam was made a living soul but the last Adam was made a quickening spirit.

And so it is written, The first man Adam was made a living soul; the last Adam was made a quickening spirit.

1 Corinthians 15:45

The word "spirit" in 1 Corinthians 15:45 is the Greek word "pneuma" which means *"a breath, the Holy Ghost or a divine God."* This scripture clearly shows that the Holy Spirit is God Almighty.

Chapter 3

JESUS AND THE HOLY SPIRIT

The Holy Spirit worked with the Lord Jesus for the success of His ministry right from the throne room of heaven to the earth. This tells us how important the Holy Spirit is to the believer, especially if we are to do well in serving Christ.

The Holy Spirit Transformed Jesus into a Man

And without controversy great is the mystery of godliness: God was manifest in the flesh, justified in the Spirit, seen of angels, preached unto the Gentiles, believed on in the world, received up into glory.

1 Timothy 3:16

Jesus Christ was God who became a man. He was a total man while on the earth and that is why the word of God calls Him the son of man.

And Jesus saith unto him, The foxes have holes, and the birds of the air have nests; but the Son of man hath not where to lay his head.

Matthew 8:20

In fact, God the Holy Spirit took God the Son who is a Spirit and transformed Him into a total man on the earth. When the angel of the Lord appeared to Mary with the message that she was going to give birth to a son, she was a virgin. We all know that it is impossible for a virgin to be pregnant without a man. That is why Mary asked *"how shall this be?"* Glory be to Jesus that with God all things are possible (Mark 10:27).

Then said Mary unto the angel, How shall this be, seeing I know not a man?

And the angel answered and said unto her, The Holy Ghost shall come upon thee, and the power of the Highest shall overshadow thee: therefore also that holy thing which shall be born of thee shall be called the Son of God.

Luke 1:34-35

The moment the Holy Ghost came upon Mary, Jesus who was a Spirit in heaven, was instantly transformed into a man with a body in the womb of Mary. This is what I call true power!

Wherefore when he cometh into the world, he saith, Sacrifice and offering thou wouldest not, but a body hast thou prepared me.

Hebrews 10:5

The Holy Spirit is the power of the Godhead and His power is limitless. This is how He took God who is a Spirit and transformed Him into a man. It is the greatest miracle that ever took place upon the earth, that God the creator of the heavens and earth became human, just like us.

The Holy Spirit Empowered Jesus To Teach, Preach, Heal, Cast out devils and Raise the dead

Jesus was a total man. Therefore, His ministry would not have started without the help of the Holy Spirit. When you read through the gospels, we never see Jesus teaching, preaching and healing until the coming of the Holy Spirit upon His life. As soon as the Holy Spirit came upon Him, His ministry started in a very dramatic way. The Holy Spirit first came upon Jesus while He was being baptised by John in the river Jordan.

And Jesus, when he was baptized, went up straightway out of the water: and, lo, the heavens were opened unto him, and he saw the Spirit of God descending like a dove, and lighting upon him:

And lo a voice from heaven, saying, This is my beloved Son, in whom I am well pleased.

Matthew 3:16-17

In Luke 4:1, the word of God states that Jesus Christ was full of the Holy Ghost.

And Jesus being full of the Holy Ghost returned from Jordan, and was led by the Spirit into the wilderness.

Luke 4:1

Jesus returned from Jordan in the power of the Holy Ghost and entered into Galilee to teach, preach and to heal.

And Jesus returned in the power of the Spirit into Galilee: and there went out a fame of him through all the region round about.

Luke 4:14

This is when His ministry actually began. His ministry began with the power of the Holy Ghost.

And Jesus went about all Galilee, teaching in their synagogues, and preaching the gospel of the kingdom, and healing all manner of sickness and all manner of disease among the people.
And his fame went throughout all Syria: and they brought unto him all sick people that were taken with divers diseases and torments, and those which were possessed with devils, and those which were lunatick, and those that had the palsy; and he healed them.

And there followed him great multitudes of people from Galilee, and from Decapolis, and from Jerusalem, and from Judaea, and from beyond Jordan.

Matthew 4:23-25

Without the Holy Spirit, Jesus would not have been able to teach, preach, heal the sick, raise the dead and cast out devils. Jesus would not have been able to perform all the miracles He performed because He was a total man. He needed the anointing of the Holy Ghost to perform those miracles. The Pharisees even started to accuse Jesus and say that He must be casting out devils by using evil powers. Jesus answered them firmly that devils are cast out by the power of the Holy Ghost.

But if I cast out devils by the Spirit of God, then the kingdom of God is come unto you.

Matthew 12:28

Jesus emphatically said that it is the Spirit of God that enabled Him to do such mighty works while on the earth.

The Spirit of the Lord is upon me, because he hath anointed me to preach the gospel to the poor; he hath sent me to heal the brokenhearted, to preach deliverance to the captives, and recovering of sight to the blind, to set at liberty them that are bruised,

To preach the acceptable year of the Lord.

Luke 4:18-19

Jesus was anointed with the Holy Ghost and with power.

How God anointed Jesus of Nazareth with the Holy Ghost and with power: who went about doing good, and healing all that were oppressed of the devil; for God was with him.

Acts 10:38

The Holy Spirit Raised Jesus from the Dead

Without the Holy Spirit, there will be no Christianity. If you ever enter into a church where the Holy Spirit is not present, run out because you will die spiritually with the pastor of that church. The Holy Spirit is the founder, foundation and the builder of the church.

Is it not amazing that, if the Holy Ghost had not raised Jesus from the dead, He would still be in the grave now! The death and resurrection of Jesus Christ is the main proof for Christianity. If Jesus did not rise from the grave then our faith is in vain and not valid.

And if Christ be not risen, then is our preaching vain, and your faith is also vain.

1 Corinthians 15:14

But thanks be to God for the blessed Holy Spirit who by His power raised Jesus up from the grave. Jesus is no more in the grave, He is risen!

He is not here: for he is risen, as he said. Come, see the place where the Lord lay.

Matthew 28:6

The grave could not hold Him captive because of the power of the Holy Ghost.

But if the Spirit of him that raised up Jesus from the dead dwell in you, he that raised up Christ from the dead shall also quicken your mortal bodies by his Spirit that dwelleth in you.

Romans 8:11

The Holy Spirit Took Jesus Back to Heaven

Jesus completed His redemption work on the cross by the power of the Holy Spirit. After it was completed, the Holy Spirit took Him back to heaven. The Holy Spirit brought Jesus to the earth, anointed Him to do the ministry work, raised Him from the dead and took Him back to heaven. The Holy Spirit is the cloud that took Jesus to Heaven.

And when he had spoken these things, while they beheld, he was taken up; and a cloud received him out of their sight.

And while they looked stedfastly toward heaven as he went up, behold, two men stood by them in white apparel;

Which also said, Ye men of Galilee, why stand ye gazing up into heaven? this same Jesus, which is taken up from you into heaven, shall so come in

like manner as ye have seen him go into heaven.

Acts 1:9-11

Jesus Stressed the Importance of the Holy Spirit

The man Christ Jesus was limited because He could only be at one place at a time. He had to walk from one city to another to spread the gospel. But the Holy Ghost is omnipresent which means He can be everywhere at the same time. Think about it. Every Sunday morning, millions of people worldwide gather to worship the Lord and the Holy Spirit fellowships with all of these believers. Jesus could not have done so as a man. That is why He told the disciples that He had to go so that the Holy Spirit could be given to everyone for the perfecting of the work of the kingdom.

Nevertheless I tell you the truth; It is expedient for you that I go away: for if I go not away, the Comforter will not come unto you; but if I depart, I will send him unto you.

John 16:7

Father in the mighty name of Jesus,
I pray that the power of the Holy Spirit,
which manifested in the life of Jesus, will
manifest in my life.
Let Your will for my life manifest because
of the blessed Holy Spirit in my life.
In Jesus name, Amen.

***

Chapter 4

THE WORK OF THE HOLY SPIRIT

The work of the Holy Spirit is unique and special. We cannot do the work of God without the Holy Spirit because He is the one who injects life into the work of God. A church without the Holy Spirit is a dead church, a Christian without the Holy Spirit is a lifeless Christian and the Bible without the Holy Spirit is just another story book without power. In fact, the word of God without the Holy Spirit and His power behind it will not work.

A believer cannot live the Christian life without the help of the blessed Holy Spirit. In fact, no one can be a Christian and know God and His word without the Holy Spirit. A pastor devoid of the Holy Spirit is doomed for failure. If Jesus Christ fulfilled His ministry by the help of the Holy Spirit, then every true minister of the gospel cannot do God's work without the Holy Spirit.

Let's take a look at five major works of the Holy Spirit.

Conviction and Salvation

No one can convert a person who is not saved just by speaking. Salvation is purely the work of the Holy Spirit. You can preach like fire to an unsaved person but if the Holy Spirit does not convict that person, your preaching of fire will be in vain. Christians who enter into relationships with unbelievers with the aim of converting them to the Lord truly deceive themselves.

Salvation is of the heart and only the Holy Spirit can do this work of salvation in a person. Jesus Himself told His disciples that salvation belongs to the Holy Spirit.

Nevertheless I tell you the truth; It is expedient for you that I go away: for if I go not away, the Comforter will not come unto you; but if I depart, I will send him unto you.

And when he is come, he will reprove the world of sin, and of righteousness, and of judgment:

Of sin, because they believe not on me;

Of righteousness, because I go to my Father, and ye see me no more;

Of judgment, because the prince of this world is judged.
John 16:7-11

It is one thing to preach and it is another thing for the person to be convicted by the word of God. It is the blessed Holy Spirit who causes conviction to take place in the heart of the unsaved person. Before salvation, the Holy Spirit is with the unbeliever to convict them of their sins and turn their heart to the Lord.

How does a hardened criminal break down and start weeping because he now acknowledges that he is a sinner and needs the forgiveness of the Lord? It is the Holy Spirit who massages the word of God into the heart and allows the word to penetrate into the heart of the unsaved. The Holy Spirit causes the word of God to prick the heart of the unsaved and cause salvation to take place.

After the disciples had preached, the Holy Spirit caused the word of God to cut through the hearts of the people and convict them of their sins. And as soon as they were convicted, they began to ask the disciples what they could do to obtain salvation.

Now when they heard this, they were pricked in their heart, and said unto Peter and to the rest of the apostles, Men and brethren, what shall we do?
Acts 2:37

Guidance

In the Old Testament, when people needed guidance, they went to see a prophet. This is because those in the Old Testament were not born again and did not have the Holy Spirit. Only the kings, priests and prophets had the Holy Spirit. For instance, when Saul was looking for his father's lost donkey, he went to see Prophet Samuel to know where the donkey could be found. They sought guidance from the prophets.

And he said unto him, Behold now, there is in this city a man of God, and he is an honourable man; all that he saith cometh surely to pass: now let us go thither; peradventure he can shew us our way that we should go.

Then said Saul to his servant, But, behold, if we go, what shall we bring the man? for the bread is spent in our vessels, and there is not a present to bring to the man of God: what have we?

And the servant answered Saul again, and said, Behold, I have here at hand the fourth part of a shekel of silver: that will I give to the man of God, to tell us our way.

(Beforetime in Israel, when a man went to enquire of God, thus he spake, Come, and let us go to the seer: for he that is now called a Prophet was beforetime called a Seer.)

1 Samuel 9:6-9

The prophetic ministry is very important in the present day body of Christ but Christians are to no longer seek guidance from a prophet. They are to be guided by the Holy Spirit. Jesus said that when the Holy Spirit comes, He will guide us into all truth. "To guide" means *"to show the way and to lead."* The children of God need the leadership of the Holy Spirit.

How be it when he the Spirit of truth, is come, he will guide you into all truth; for he shall not speak of himself; but whatsoever he shall hear, that shall he speak: and he will show you things to come.

John 16:13

Many Christians are led by money, lust and the desires of the flesh. This is why there is such chaos and confusion in the body of Christ. There are even some churches which are led by the spirit of the world instead of the Holy Spirit of God. The spirit of the world is the spirit that causes pastors to preach only prosperity messages to God's people. The spirit of the world causes Christians to be only earthly minded and not spiritually minded. The spirit of the world causes believers to seek only material blessings and not spiritual blessings. The spirit of the world causes churches and Christians to forget about the lost and the unsaved souls. But the Bible says that those who are led by the Spirit of God are the true children of God.

For as many as are led by the Spirit of God, they are the sons of God.

Romans 8:14

I urge you to seek the guidance of the Holy Spirit in all your decision making. Never take a decision without a confirmation from the Holy Spirit. If you want to marry, pray to God about it and seek the guidance of the Holy Spirit in order for God to give you the right husband or wife. Every step we take must be guided by the Holy Spirit.

Do not choose your marriage partner before praying about it. Many Christians only start praying to God to confirm their choice after they have set eyes on the person they want to marry. When you do this, you are only asking God to stamp what you have already chosen. God will surely guide you to make the right choice so you do not become a prisoner in your own house.

I see the Holy Spirit guiding you right now to remove any confusion in your life. You are at a crossroad now and you are confused about which direction to go.

But I am announcing to you right now that the Holy Spirit is stepping into that decision! He is providing you with guidance and answers.

Listen carefully, He is speaking to you right now. He will lead and guide you. In Jesus name. Amen.

Teaching

The Spirit of God is the author of the Bible and He is the best person to teach us. I have heard people say that the Bible contradicts itself but this is not so. The Bible will only seem to contradict itself to the reader if the reader is not being taught the word by the Holy Spirit.

I was once talking to a gentleman who said he was a theologian. This theologian said he did not understand the reason why we Christians have to pray. He also said that once saved, you are always saved and that God has forgiven us of our past sins, present sins and future sins. He continued to explain that because we are now under grace, you can continue in sin and you will still go to heaven. This theologian is completely devoid of the Holy Spirit. He has clearly not allowed the Holy Spirit to teach him His word. The fact that you know the Bible from Genesis to Revelation does not mean that you understand it. You have just accumulated knowledge without the Holy Spirit. This kind of knowledge is just like having knowledge from an academic text book. The word of God can only be interpreted correctly by the help of the Holy Spirit and it can only be understood by the help of the Holy Spirit.

First of all, the word of God says that we should call unto Him and He will answer us.

Call unto me, and I will answer thee, and show thee great and mighty things, which thou knowest not.

Jeremiah 33:3

The word of God also says that we should ask and we will receive. Which means if we do not call, we will not receive an answer and if we do not ask God for our needs, we will not receive them.

Ask, and it shall be given you; seek, and ye shall find; knock, and it shall be opened unto you.

Matthew 7:7

Secondly, once saved does not mean always saved. If you are a Christian and you continue in sin and you die in your sins, you will go to hell just like all sinners. Paul asked if we should continue in sin since grace abounds. He answered and said, God forbid.

What shall we say then? Shall we continue in sin, that grace may abound?

God forbid. How shall we, that are dead to sin, live any longer therein?

Romans 6:1-2

Thirdly, if you do not ask for forgiveness of sins, you shall not be forgiven. The word of God says that if we confess our sins, our God is faithful and just to forgive us and cleanse us from all unrighteousness.

If we confess our sins, he is faithful and just to forgive us our sins, and to cleanse us from all unrighteousness.

1 John 1:9

Any time we open the Bible, we must ask the Holy Spirit to teach us His word. David asked the Lord to open His eyes to the wondrous things in the word of God.

Open thou mine eyes, that I may behold wondrous things out of thy law.

Psalm 119:18

The Holy Spirit will teach us and guide us into all truth. The Bible says that knowing the truth shall set you free.

And ye shall know the truth, and the truth shall make you free.

John 8:32

But this truth will not come to us without the Holy Spirit. In John 14:26, Jesus said that when the Holy Spirit comes, He will teach us.

But the Comforter, which is the Holy Ghost, whom the Father will send in my name, he will teach you

all things and bring all things to your remembrance, whatsoever I have said unto you.

John 14:26

The word "teach" in this scripture means *"to learn."* We are to learn from the Holy Spirit the word of the living God. 1 John 2:27 also says that the Holy Spirit is in us in the form of the anointing to teach us all things.

But the anointing which ye have received of him abideth in you, and ye need not that any man teach you: but as the same anointing teacheth you of all things, and is truth, and is no lie, and even as it hath taught you, ye shall abide in him.

1 John 2:27

Revelation

The Holy Spirit is the spirit of revelation. The word "reveal" means *"to take off the cover, to discover and to disclose."* We uncover something that is covered, we discover something that is hidden and we disclose something that is secret. It is therefore the work of the Holy Spirit to uncover the word of God to Christians, to enable believers to discover the hidden things of the kingdom of God and to find the secret things of God.

Without the Holy Spirit, we will not experience the supernatural. The blessed Holy Spirit opens our spiritual eyes to see into the spiritual realm. When I became born again, the Holy Spirit revealed the word of God to me and He also revealed my future to me. Many people have asked me, what is the purpose of God for their lives? But if they will only turn to the Holy Spirit, it shall be revealed to them. People live for many years and some even die without knowing the plan of God for their lives but it shall not be your portion! Ask the Holy Spirit to reveal to you what you are supposed to do in this life. Specifically pray to God for Him to reveal your future to you and allow His will to be done in your life.

But as it is written, Eye hath not seen, nor ear heard, neither have entered into the heart of man, the things which God hath prepared for them that love him.

But God hath revealed them unto us by his Spirit: for the Spirit searcheth all things, yea, the deep things of God.

For what man knoweth the things of a man, save the spirit of man which is in him? even so the things of God knoweth no man, but the Spirit of God.

1 Corinthians 2:9-11

The language of the Holy Spirit includes the supernatural manifestation of dreams and visions. These are other forms of revelations. The word of God says that He will show us things to come.

Howbeit when he, the Spirit of truth, is come, he will guide you into all truth: for he shall not speak of himself; but whatsoever he shall hear, that shall he speak: and he will shew you things to come.

John 16:13

The Holy Spirit shows us things to come through dreams and visions.

And it shall come to pass in the last days, saith God, I will pour out of my Spirit upon all flesh: and your sons and your daughters shall prophesy, and your young men shall see visions, and your old men shall dream dreams:

And on my servants and on my handmaidens I will pour out in those days of my Spirit; and they shall prophesy:

Acts 2:17-18

From today, start praying to the Lord to reveal His word to you. He will surely reveal His purpose for your life through the blessed Holy Spirit.

Witnessing or Testifying or Evangelism

For us to be effective witnesses of the gospel, we must co-operate with the Holy Spirit. He is the power, the force, the drive and the impetus behind evangelism. If souls are to be saved on a larger scale, we must call upon the Spirit of God.

But ye shall receive power, after that the Holy Ghost is come upon you: and ye shall be witnesses unto me both in Jerusalem, and in all Judaea, and in Samaria, and unto the uttermost part of the earth.

Acts 1:8

Christians can witness and testify effectively with the help of the Holy Ghost. It is the Holy Spirit speaking through us that will cause an unsaved soul to be saved. Jesus said that the Holy Spirit will testify of Him.

Before you go for evangelism, pray that the Holy Spirit will speak through you and that the Holy Spirit will save the lost. When we refuse to heed to the guidance and leading of the Holy Spirit, we enter into all sorts of arguments with the people we are witnessing to. Arguments will not save the lost. Arguements will harden their hearts to not listen to the word you are preaching. Allow the Holy Spirit to testify through you because He is the Spirit of testimony and the greatest evangelist. Indeed Jesus said the Holy Spirit shall testify of Him.

But when the Comforter is come, whom I will send unto you from the Father, even the Spirit of truth, which proceedeth from the Father, he shall testify of me:

John 15:26

Dear Holy Spirit,
I ask You to convict me when I am going the wrong way.
I ask You to guide me into the truth of God's word.
Teach me and reveal the word of God to me.
Open my eyes to see dreams and visions and empower me to be an effective witness for Jesus.
In Jesus name, Amen.

Chapter 5

THE ABIDING PRESENCE OF THE HOLY SPIRIT AND THE BELIEVER

The Spirit of God dwells with the believer in three ways. He abides *inside* the believer, He abides *upon* the believer and He abides *with* the believer. Each of these three ways by which the Spirit of God abides with the believer have powerful effects. The believer must know these three ways and be conscious of the abiding presence of the Holy Spirit.

The Holy Spirit *In* Us

The first way by which the Holy Spirit abides with the believer is by dwelling or residing inside the believer.

Know ye not that ye are the temple of God, and that the Spirit of God dwelleth in you?

1 Corinthians 3:16

And what agreement hath the temple of God with idols? For ye are the temple of the living God; as God hath said, I will dwell in them, and walk in them; and I will be their God, and they shall be my people.

2 Corinthians 6:16

Every believer receives the Holy Spirit at the point of salvation. The Spirit of God therefore abides in everyone who is born again. This means that, without the abiding presence of the Holy Spirit, a person cannot be a child of God.

But ye are not in the flesh, but in the Spirit, if so be that the Spirit of God dwell in you. Now if any man has not the Spirit of Christ, he is none of his.

Romans 8:9

How do you know that you are saved? It is the Spirit of God abiding within us that convinces us that we are the children of God. He, the blessed Holy Spirit, bears witness with our spirit that we are the children of God. So in effect, we know that we know without a shadow of doubt, that we are the children of God because of the abiding presence of the Holy Spirit.

The Spirit itself beareth witness with our spirit, that we are the children of God.

Romans 8:16

The word of God also states that whosoever receives Jesus Christ has been given the power to become the child of God. This power, authority and right to become God's child is as a result of the Holy Spirit within the believer.

But as many as received him, to them gave he power to become the sons of God, even to them that believe on his name.

John 1:12

As soon as you become born again, the Holy Spirit resides within your spirit and makes you one with Jesus Christ.

But he that is joined unto the Lord is one spirit.

1 Corinthians 6:17

Furthermore, in order to know the truth of God's word, it has to be revealed to you by the Holy Spirit.

The Holy Spirit has to reveal and teach you the word of God, otherwise you will not understand it.

But the Comforter, which is the Holy Ghost, whom the Father will send in my name, he shall teach you all things, and bring all things to your remembrance, whatsoever I have said unto you.

John 14:26

But the anointing which ye have received of him abideth in you, and ye need not that any man teach you: but as the same anointing teacheth you of all things, and is truth, and is no lie, and even as it hath taught you, ye shall abide in him.

1 John 2:27

I once had a work colleague who was not saved and one day he began to argue with me about the word of God and how he thought it contradicted itself. So I turned to him and said that we cannot use our finite mind to interpret the word of God. The Bible is not a story book. It is a spiritual book with a spiritual author who is God and you need spiritual enlightenment given by the Holy Ghost to understand it. Your spiritual eyes must be opened, otherwise you will not understand the word of God.

That the God of our Lord Jesus Christ, the Father of glory, may give unto you the spirit of wisdom and revelation in the knowledge of him:

The eyes of your understanding being enlightened; that ye may know what is the hope of his calling, and what the riches of the glory of his inheritance in the saints.

Ephesians 1:17-18

That is why King David prayed for the Lord to open his eyes that he may behold wondrous things out of the word of God.

Open thou mine eyes, that I may behold wondrous things out of thy law.

Psalm 119:18

Moreover, the Spirit of God indwells in the believer to teach the believer the truth of God's word. The word of God states that the Holy Spirit will guide you into all truth.

Howbeit when he, the Spirit of truth, is come, he will guide you into all truth: for he shall not speak of himself; but whatsoever he shall hear, that shall he speak: and he will shew you things to come.

John 16:13

Finally, the Holy Spirit indwells in us to enable us to give God sweet worship. The word of God states that God is a Spirit and they that worship Him must worship Him in Spirit and in truth. This is made possible by the Holy Ghost that lives in us.

And because ye are sons, God hath sent forth the Spirit of his son into your hearts, crying, Abba, Father.

Galatians 4:6

For ye have not received the spirit of bondage again to fear; but ye have received the Spirit of adoption, whereby we cry, Abba, Father.

Romans 8:15

The Holy Spirit *Upon* Us

The second way by which the Holy Spirit abides with the believer is by being upon the person. The purpose of the Holy Spirit coming upon a believer is to transform, to move, to empower, to enable, to perform, to act, to work, to overcome and to speak boldly. In other words, the Holy Spirit comes upon a believer for service. When the Lord calls you to serve Him, He anoints you with His Spirit. That is when the Holy Spirit comes upon you, to enable you to do what the Lord has called you to do or accomplish. Without the Holy Spirit upon you, you are not empowered to do ministry work. That is why Jesus told His disciples to wait for the Holy Spirit, so that they would be endued with power from on high.

And, behold, I send the promise of my Father upon you: but tarry ye in the city of Jerusalem, until ye be endued with power from on high.

Luke 24:49

Without the Spirit upon you, no one can do effective ministry work. No one can be an effective witness for the Lord. The Spirit of the Lord came upon the disciples to make them effective witnesses for the Lord.

But ye shall receive power, after that the Holy Ghost is come upon you and ye shall be witnesses unto me both in Jerusalem, and in all Judea, and in Samaria, and unto the uttermost part of the earth.

Acts 1:8

The disciples received boldness to speak His word after receiving the Holy Spirit.

And when they had prayed, the place was shaken where they were assembled together; and they were

all filled with the Holy Ghost, and they spake the word of God with boldness.

Acts 4:31

Even our Saviour Jesus Christ had to wait for the Spirit upon Him to begin His ministry. The Spirit upon is the anointing to serve, to break yokes, to destroy evil, to free people, to raise the dead, to heal the sick, to cleanse lepers and to preach the gospel. Jesus said:

The Spirit of the Lord is upon me, because he hath anointed me to preach the gospel to the poor; he hath sent me to heal the brokenhearted, to preach deliverance to the captives, and recovering of sight to the blind, to set at liberty them that are bruised,

To preach the acceptable year of the Lord.

Luke 4:18-19

Every believer must therefore long for the Spirit of the Lord to come upon them so they can do the good works that we have been created to do.

For we are his workmanship, created in Christ Jesus unto good works, which God hath before ordained that we should walk in them.

Ephesians 2:10

We must continue the good works that Jesus did the good works that the apostles accomplished. The only way to do this is for the Holy Spirit to come upon us. Another dimension of the Holy Spirit upon us is that He is rubbed or smeared like a balm on us. This is what is called the anointing.

To be "anointed" means *"to be rubbed or smeared with the Holy Ghost and power."* The power is as a result of the Holy Spirit coming upon us. God is the one who anoints people to do His work. His main ingredient for anointing the saints is with the Holy Ghost and power.

How God anointed Jesus of Nazareth with the Holy Ghost and with power: who went about doing good, and healing all that were oppressed of the devil; for God was with him.

Acts 10:38

The Old Testament is full of people whom the Spirit of the Lord came upon. It enabled them to accomplish what the Lord required of them. Some of these people were fearful people but when the Spirit of the Lord came upon them, they did unusual things for the Lord. They became mighty and accomplished much for the Lord.

Without the Holy Spirit, nothing can be done.

Let's look at some of the people in the Old Testament whom the Spirit of God came upon.

Samson

And the Spirit of the Lord began to move him at times in the camp of Dan between Zorah and Eshtaol.

Judges 13:25

And Samson went down to Timnath, and saw a woman in Timnath of the daughters of the Philistines.

And he came up, and told his father and his mother, and said, I have seen a woman in Timnath of the daughters of the Philistines: now therefore get her for me to wife.

Then his father and his mother said unto him, Is there never a woman among the daughters of thy brethren, or among all my people, that thou goest to take a wife of the uncircumcised Philistines? And Samson said unto his father, Get her for me; for she pleaseth me well.

But his father and his mother knew not that it was of the LORD, that he sought an occasion against the Philistines: for at that time the Philistines had dominion over Israel.

Then went Samson down, and his father and his mother, to Timnath, and came to the vineyards of Timnath: and, behold, a young lion roared against him.

And the Spirit of the LORD came mightily upon him, and he rent him as he would have rent a kid, and he had nothing in his hand: but he told not his father or his mother what he had done.

Judges 14:1-6

And the Spirit of the LORD came upon him, and he went down to Ashkelon, and slew thirty men of them, and took their spoil, and gave change of garments unto them which expounded the riddle. And his anger was kindled, and he went up to his father's house.

Judges 14:19

Othniel

Therefore the anger of the LORD was hot against Israel, and he sold them into the hand of Chushanrishathaim king of Mesopotamia: and the children of Israel served Chushanrishathaim eight years.

And when the children of Israel cried unto the LORD, the LORD raised up a deliverer to the children of

Israel, who delivered them, even Othniel the son of Kenaz, Caleb's younger brother.

And the Spirit of the LORD came upon him, and he judged Israel, and went out to war: and the LORD delivered Chushanrishathaim king of Mesopotamia into his hand; and his hand prevailed against Chushanrishathaim.

Judges 3:8-10

Gideon

But the Spirit of the Lord came upon Gideon, and he blew a trumpet; and Abiezer was gathered after him.

Judges 6:34

Saul

And the Spirit of the Lord will come upon thee, and thou shalt prophesy with them, and shalt be turned into another man.

1 Samuel 10:6

David

Then Samuel took the horn of oil, and anointed him in the midst of his bretheren and the Spirit of the Lord came upon David from that day forward. So Samuel rose up, and went to Ramah.

1 Samuel 16:13

Azariah the Son of Oded

And the Spirit of God came upon Azariah the son of Oded.

And he went out to meet Asa, and said unto him, Hear ye me, Asa, and all Judah and Benjamin; The LORD is with you, while ye be with him; and if ye seek him, he will be found of you; but if ye forsake him, he will forsake you.

2 Chronicles 15:1-2

Jahaziel the Son of Zechariah

Then upon Jahaziel the son of Zechariah, the son of Benaiah, the son of Jeiel, the son of Mattaniah, a Levite of the sons of Asaph, came the Spirit of the LORD in the midst of the congregation;

And he said, Hearken ye, all Judah, and ye inhabitants of Jerusalem, and thou king Jehoshaphat, Thus saith the LORD unto you, Be not afraid nor dismayed by reason of this great multitude; for the battle is not yours, but God's.

To morrow go ye down against them: behold, they come up by the cliff of Ziz; and ye shall find them at the end of the brook, before the wilderness of Jeruel.

2 Chronicles 20:14-16

The Holy Spirit *With* Us

The third way that the Spirit of God abides with the believer is to be with the Christian.

And I will pray the Father, and he shall give you another Comforter, that he may abide with you for ever;

Even the Spirit of truth; whom the world cannot receive, because it seeth him not, neither knoweth him: but ye know him; for he dwelleth with you, and shall be in you.

John 14:16-17

The purpose of the Holy Spirit with us is to lead us, guide us, show us the ways of God and teach us His will.

For as many as are led by the Spirit of God, they are the sons of God.

Romans 8:14

Christians today are eagerly seeking after miracles but they are not seeking to know the God who is the worker of these miracles. We must pray like Moses did, that God will show us His ways. The word of God tells us that Moses knew the ways of God but the children of Israel knew only His acts. The acts of God are the miracles that God performs in the lives of His children.

But Moses did not only want to see the miracles and the power of God. He prayed earnestly for God to show him His ways.

Now therefore, I pray thee, if I have found grace in thy sight, shew me now thy way, that I may know thee, that I may find grace in thy sight: and consider that this nation is thy people.

And he said, My presence shall go with thee, and I will give thee rest.

Exodus 33:13-14

Moses received an answer for what he prayed for.

He made known his ways unto Moses, his acts unto the children of Israel.

Psalm 103:7

David, who was a man after God's heart, also prayed this prayer in the book of Psalms. He wanted to know God and to please Him.

Shew me thy ways, O Lord, teach me thy paths.
Psalm 25:4

Teach me thy way, O Lord, and lead me in a plain path, because of mine enemies.
Psalm 27: 11

Those who only know the acts of God will collapse in times of difficulties, trials and tribulations. But those who know His ways will stand firm. The ways of God are many. Seek to know His ways of holiness, purity, patience, forgiveness, love, giving, faith, total trust and dependency on God and so forth.

Lastly, you can talk to the Holy Spirit because He dwells with us as a person. He is not just a wind or some vapour. In fact, the Bible calls Him *"He."*

Howbeit when he, the Spirit of truth, is come, he will guide you into all truth: for he shall not speak of himself; but whatsoever he shall hear, that shall he speak: and he will shew you things to come.
John 16:13

But the Comforter, which is the Holy Ghost, whom the Father will send in my name, he shall teach you all things, and bring all things to your remembrance, whatsoever I have said unto you.

John 14:26

But when the Comforter is come, whom I will send unto you from the Father, even the Spirit of truth, which proceedeth from the Father, he shall testify of me.

John 15:26

Furthermore, the word of God states that the Holy Spirit has a mind which means He can think.

Likewise the Spirit also helpeth our infirmities: for we know not what we should pray for as we ought: but the Spirit itself maketh intercession for us with groanings which cannot be uttered.

Romans 8:26

The Holy Spirit can also be grieved.

And grieve not the holy Spirit of God, whereby ye are sealed unto the day of redemption.

Ephesians 4:30

Now, why am I mentioning all of this? I am saying all of this because the Holy Spirit is a person and you can talk to Him and communicate with Him every blessed day! One day, someone came to me very upset and told me that they were offended. This person blamed some church members for causing the offence. I remember sitting at work a few days later and thinking about the issue. So I asked the Holy Spirit, "why is this person behaving like this?" You may not believe it but after a few minutes the Holy Spirit spoke to me. He said, "this person's heart is broken because of a secret relationship." I immediately became calm as I realised that the offence was not the fault of others. It was hidden within this person's heart. When you speak to the Holy Spirit, He will show you many things and explain many things to you, including the word of God. When you read the Bible and you do not understand, ask Him to explain it to you. He is the author of the word of God and He is the best person to explain it to you. I have done this on several occasions and He has never failed to explain the word to me each and every time.

We need the Holy Spirit otherwise we cannot live the Christian life and we cannot walk the Christian walk. Without the Holy Spirit there will be no Christianity and there will be no salvation. Without the Holy Spirit we cannot do God's work. Churches devoid of the Spirit of God are destined for destruction.

We must therefore make it our greatest mission to know the Spirit of God whom the Lord has given to us as Christians.

One of the promises of God is that when we ask Him for the Holy Spirit, He will give Him to us.

And I say unto you, Ask, and it shall be given you; seek, and ye shall find; knock, and it shall be opened unto you.

For every one that asketh receiveth; and he that seeketh findeth; and to him that knocketh it shall be opened.

If a son shall ask bread of any of you that is a father, will he give him a stone? or if he ask a fish, will he for a fish give him a serpent?

Or if he shall ask an egg, will he offer him a scorpion?

If ye then, being evil, know how to give good gifts unto your children: how much more shall your heavenly Father give the Holy Spirit to them that ask him?

Luke 11:9-13

If you do not know the Holy Sprit or you do not have a relationship with Him, you can start from today.

You can ask for the Holy Spirt right now. Just say this prayer meaningfully with all your heart.

Dear Holy Spirit, I want to know you and I want you to be my friend. Please adopt me, train me, guide me, lead me and bring me up in the Lord.

Dear Father, please anoint me with your Spirit as you have said in your word so that I will be able to do the work you have called me to do.

Lord, you said you will give the Holy Spirit to them that ask. I therefore ask you to give me the Holy Spirit, in the name of Jesus. Amen.

Chapter 6

WHAT IS THE BAPTISM OF THE HOLY SPIRIT WITH THE EVIDENCE OF SPEAKING IN TONGUES?

During water baptism, a person is fully and totally immersed into water. This is very symbolic of the Holy Spirit baptism in that the person is totally and fully soaked with the Holy Spirit. Apostle John explained that Jesus Christ is the one who baptises us with the Holy Ghost.

I indeed baptize you with water unto repentance: but he that cometh after me is mightier than I, whose shoes I am

not worthy to bear: he shall baptize you with the Holy Ghost, and with fire.

Matthew 3:11

Two dramatic things happen when we are baptised with the Holy Ghost. Firstly, we are filled with the Holy Ghost to the brim with the evidence of speaking in tongues. Secondly, we receive the fire of the Holy Ghost for purification and purging.

What is Speaking in Tongues?

Speaking in tongues is the initial sign that a person is filled with the Holy Spirit. As I said earlier, when a person is baptised with the Holy Spirit, they are filled to the brim with the evidence of speaking in tongues. However, we must understand that although speaking in tongues is a gift imparted to the believer by the Holy Ghost, speaking in tongues is not the entirety of the Holy Spirit.

For instance, if I give you my phone to keep and you take it home, it does not mean that you have me at your house. You only have my phone and not me myself. We should therefore not limit the Holy Spirit to speaking in tongues. To clarify, speaking in tongues is also the same as praying in the Holy Ghost or praying in the Spirit.

Is Speaking in Tongues for Everyone?

Yes! It is written in God's precious word that it is a promise and this promise is for everyone who receives the Lord Jesus into their life.

It is a Gift and We Do Not All Receive the Same Gift so How Can it Be for Everyone?

The gift of speaking in tongues is the only gift I have seen in the word of God that the Father has promised to give to all His children. Every Christian must therefore have a strong desire to receive this gift.

Then Peter said unto them, Repent, and be baptized every one of you in the name of Jesus Christ for the remission of sins, and ye shall receive the gift of the Holy Ghost. For the promise is unto you, and to your children, and to all that are afar off, even as many as the Lord our God shall call.

Acts 2:38-39

The Lord Jesus also said that speaking in tongues is a sign that will follow all those who believe in Him. Jesus said that, in His name, all those who believe in Him will speak with new tongues. This makes speaking in tongues available to all those who believe and are Christians.

And these signs shall follow them that believe; In my name shall they cast out devils; they shall speak with new tongues.

Mark 16:17

Apostle Peter experienced how the Holy Ghost was poured on the Gentiles and they spoke with new tongues.

And they of the circumcision which believed were astonished, as many as came with Peter, because that on the Gentiles also was poured out the gift of the Holy Ghost.

For they heard them speak with tongues, and magnify God.

Then answered Peter, Can any man forbid water, that these should not be baptized, which have received the Holy Ghost as well as we?

Acts 10:45-47

There is a lot of confusion about speaking in tongues in the body of Christ but this confusion is as a result of misinterpretation of the holy word of God. To say that tongues is of the devil is a blasphemy against the Holy Spirit and the word of God declares that blasphemy against the Holy Ghost is a sin which shall never be forgiven.

Wherefore I say unto you, All manner of sin and blasphemy shall be forgiven unto men: but the blasphemy against the Holy Ghost shall not be forgiven unto men.

Matthew 12:31

Even Apostle Paul who wrote more than half of the New Testament said in 1 Corinthians 14:18;

I thank my God, I speak with tongues more than ye all.
1 Corinthians 14:18

So how can some churches and some 'so called' Christians deny speaking in tongues and call it something that is of the devil? The Lord Jesus asked the disciples to wait for the promise of the Father.

And, behold, I send the promise of my Father upon you: but tarry ye in the city of Jerusalem, until ye be endued with power from on high.

Luke 24:49

In Acts chapter 2, we can see that this promise was fulfilled.

And when the day of Pentecost was fully come, they were all with one accord in one place.

And suddenly there came a sound from heaven as of a rushing mighty wind, and it filled all the house where they were sitting.

And there appeared unto them cloven tongues like as of fire, and it sat upon each of them.

And they were all filled with the Holy Ghost, and began to speak with other tongues, as the Spirit gave them utterance.
Acts 2:1-4

You can see from this passage of scripture that the disciples began to speak in tongues as the Spirit of God gave them utterance. It was the Holy Spirit who gave them this gift and it was the same Holy Spirit who enabled them to speak. Speaking in tongues is not of the devil but of the Holy Spirit of God. Amen.

EXPLANATION OF SPEAKING IN TONGUES FROM 1 CORINTHIANS CHAPTER 14

In order to remove any doubt or confusion about speaking in tongues that satan has plagued the body of Christ with, we are going to study it step by step using key scriptures from 1 Corinthians 14:1-40.

Follow after charity, and desire spiritual gifts, but

rather that ye may prophesy.

1 Corinthians 14:1

In this opening verse, the word of God is encouraging us to follow charity, better known as love, and to also desire spiritual gifts. This is because Christians tend to not desire spiritual gifts but rather desire to have material things. The verse also goes on to say that we should desire even to prophesy. God is encouraging us, that in addition to the spiritual gifts, we must desire also to prophesy.

For he that speaketh in an unknown tongue speaketh not unto men, but unto God: for no man understandeth him; howbeit in the spirit he speaketh mysteries.

1 Corinthians 14:2

When we speak in tongues, no human being understands us unless the Holy Spirit allows them to understand so that they can interpret. This is the reason why the devil does not want Christians to speak in tongues. The devil does not understand the language of tongues and he cannot interpret it. He is not able to understand our prayers so he makes plans to negate and hinder them when we speak in tongues. When we speak in tongues, we speak in a language only God understands and we speak mysteries in the Spirit. Christians must therefore pray most of their prayers in tongues.

But he that prophesieth speaketh unto men to edification, and exhortation, and comfort.

1 Corinthians 14:3

The word "prophesieth" in 1 Corinthians 14:3 means *"to speak under inspiration"* which suggests preaching or teaching the word of God under inspiration. When you preach or speak under inspiration, you edify, exhort and comfort the whole congregation. This is because the prophecy is spoken in a normal human language that everyone can understand.

He that speaketh in an unknown tongue edifieth himself; but he that prophesieth edifieth the church.

1 Corinthians 14:4

When you speak in tongues no one understands you, it is only God who understands, but when you prophesy everyone understands. For example, if a person gets up in a church and starts to speak in tongues, nobody in the congregation would understand whatever was being spoken. But if that same person had spoken in their understanding, the congregation will understand and they will be edified.

There are, it may be, so many kinds of voices in the

world, and none of them is without signification.

1 Corinthians 14:10

Therefore if I know not the meaning of the voice, I shall be unto him that speaketh a barbarian, and he that speaketh shall be a barbarian unto me.

1 Corinthians 14:11

Even so ye, forasmuch as ye are zealous of spiritual gifts, seek that ye may excel to the edifying of the church.

1 Corinthians 14:12

Wherefore let him that speaketh in an unknown tongue pray that he may interpret.

1 Corinthians 14:13

What the above passage of scripture is saying is that when you speak in an unknown tongue in the presence of others, you will seem like a stranger because no one will understand what you are saying.

The word of God therefore encourages us in this verse of scripture to interpret what has been spoken. There is a gift of interpretation of tongues that allows tongues to be interpreted.

To another the working of miracles; to another prophecy; to another discerning of spirits; to another

divers kinds of tongues; to another the interpretation of tongues.

1 Corinthians 12:10

This gift is also imparted to the believer by the Holy Ghost. As we study the scriptures further, this point will be clearly explained.

For if I pray in an unknown tongue, my spirit prayeth, but my understanding is unfruitful.

1 Corinthians 14:14

What is it then? I will pray with the spirit, and I will pray with the understanding also: I will sing with the spirit, and I will sing with the understanding also.

1 Corinthians 14:15

Else when thou shalt bless with the spirit, how shall he that occupieth the room of the unlearned say Amen at thy giving of thanks, seeing he understandeth not what thou sayest?

1 Corinthians 14:16

For thou verily givest thanks well, but the other is not edified.

1 Corinthians 14:17

When you pray in tongues, your spirit is the one who is praying as the Holy Spirit enables your spirit. Your mind however, cannot understand what is being spoken. Do not try to understand what you are saying when speaking in tongues because no man understands it as you are speaking directly to God in a language only He understands. However, if God wills for you to understand, He will impart unto you the gift of interpretation of tongues that will enable you to understand what you are saying. When you are asked to pray in the midst of people, for example a closing prayer at the end of a service, and you pray in tongues, no one can say amen because they will not understand what you prayed. This is what the word of God is saying.

Nevertheless, you can pray in the spirit by speaking in tongues and you can also pray in your understanding in whatever language you speak. You can even sing in the spirit and you can also sing in your understanding.

I thank my God, I speak with tongues more than ye all:
1 Corinthians 14:18

Yet in the church I had rather speak five words with my understanding, that by my voice I might teach others

also, than ten thousand words in an unknown tongue.
1 Corinthians 14:19

Brethren, be not children in understanding: howbeit in malice be ye children, but in understanding be men.
1 Corinthians 14:20

In the law it is written, With men of other tongues and other lips will I speak unto this people; and yet for all that will they not hear me, saith the Lord.
1 Corinthians 14:21

Wherefore tongues are for a sign, not to them that believe, but to them that believe not: but prophesying serveth not for them that believe not, but for them which believe.
1 Corinthians 14:22

If therefore the whole church be come together into one place, and all speak with tongues, and there come in those that are unlearned, or unbelievers, will they not say that ye are mad?
1 Corinthians 14:23

But if all prophesy, and there come in one that believeth not, or one unlearned, he is convinced of all, he is judged of all:
1 Corinthians 14:24

And thus are the secrets of his heart made manifest; and so falling down on his face he will worship God, and report that God is in you of a truth.

1 Corinthians 14:25

How is it then, brethren? when ye come together, every one of you hath a psalm, hath a doctrine, hath a tongue, hath a revelation, hath an interpretation.

Let all things be done unto edifying.

1 Corinthians 14:26

If any man speak in an unknown tongue, let it be by two, or at the most by three, and that by course; and let one interpret.

1 Corinthians 14:27

But if there be no interpreter, let him keep silence in the church; and let him speak to himself, and to God.

1 Corinthians 14:28

Wherefore, brethren, covet to prophesy, and forbid not to speak with tongues.

1 Corinthians 14:39

The word of God is not saying that tongues should not be spoken in the church or speaking in tongues in the church is wrong. Paul says in verse 19, that he would rather speak five words in the church than ten thousand words in an unknown tongue. This is because if you speak in an unknown tongue to the whole church without interpretation, no one will understand what you are saying. You can speak in tongues in the church but you have to speak it to yourself. If you stand up in the congregation to speak in tongues whilst everyone is quiet, there must be an interpretation or an interpreter to interpret what has been spoken, otherwise no one will understand. It is therefore not wise to speak in tongues openly in the church when everyone is quiet and there is no interpretation.

If I go to church one day and decide to preach my sermon in tongues only, it will look foolish in the church unless there is interpretation because no one can receive the word if they do not understand. That is why Apostle Paul said that speaking five words in the church is better than speaking thousands of words in tongues. Imagine if an unbeliever enters into the church and finds everyone in the church speaking in tongues, they will not understand what is being spoken and might even run away.

One day, I was leading a church I was pastoring to pray. We were all speaking in tongues and a lady entered the church. Unfortunately, it was her first time in the church and she found all of us speaking in tongues. She stayed for about three minutes and then literally ran out of the building. I was later told that the lady said she had run out because we were all speaking strange languages. This poor lady must have had all kinds of thoughts crossing her mind at the sight of us speaking in tongues. She might have even thought that we were chanting to harm her or something.

Since that day I learnt a valuable lesson and decided that when leading prayer before a service starts, whoever is leading the prayer should pray in their understanding. This is why Apostle Paul said that, in the church, speaking in your understanding is better than speaking in tongues. He did not say this to forbid the speaking of tongues in the church but rather that all things should be done decently and in order.

In verse 27 and 28, Paul clearly states that if a person speaks in tongues in the presence of other people, there must be someone present to interpret but if there is no one to interpret then the person should keep silent. I agree with this because if there is no interpreter then it is better to speak to yourself than to speak to the hearing of the whole congregation. You can speak in tongues privately but if you speak to the hearing of the whole congregation or in the presence of others, there must be an interpretation.

When tongues are interpreted, it becomes a prophecy and therefore it exhorts, comforts and edifies the entire congregation. The word of God does not forbid tongues to be spoken in the church, it must just be done in the right context. Speaking in tongues is a gift to all of God's children and we must gladly accept it.

Chapter 7

RECEIVING THE BAPTISM OF THE HOLY SPIRIT AND SPEAKING IN TONGUES

There are two ways that people receive the gift of speaking in tongues. It can be as soon as you are filled with the Holy Ghost or by the laying on of hands. This is because some have faith more to receive than others.

TWO WAYS OF RECEIVING THE BAPTISM OF THE HOLY GHOST WITH THE EVIDENCE OF SPEAKING IN TONGUES

1. **A soon as you are filled with the Holy Ghost.**

Those with a strong desire and faith to receive this gift receive it as soon as they are filled with the Holy Ghost.

And they were all filled with the Holy Ghost, and began to speak with other tongues, as the Spirit gave them utterance.

Acts 2:4

While Peter yet spake these words, the Holy Ghost fell on all them which heard the word.

And they of the circumcision which believed were astonished, as many as came with Peter, because that on the Gentiles also was poured out the gift of the Holy Ghost.

For they heard them speak with tongues, and magnify God.

Acts 10:44-46

2. By laying on of hands.

For some believers, when hands are laid on them, it increases their faith to receive the gift of speaking in tongues. This is another effective way of receiving the gift of speaking in tongues and it is written in the Bible.

And it came to pass, that, while Apollos was at Corinth, Paul having passed through the upper coasts came to Ephesus: and finding certain disciples,

He said unto them, Have ye received the Holy Ghost since ye believed? And they said unto him, We have not so much as heard whether there be any Holy Ghost.

And he said unto them, Unto what then were ye baptized? And they said, Unto John's baptism.

Then said Paul, John verily baptized with the baptism of repentance, saying unto the people, that they should believe on him which should come after him, that is, on Christ Jesus.

When they heard this, they were baptized in the name of the Lord Jesus.

And when Paul had laid his hands upon them, the Holy Ghost came on them; and they spake with tongues, and prophesied.

Acts 19:1-6

Now when the apostles which were at Jerusalem heard that Samaria had received the word of God, they sent unto them Peter and John:

Who, when they were come down, prayed for them, that they might receive the Holy Ghost:

(For as yet he was fallen upon none of them: only they were baptized in the name of the Lord Jesus.)

Then laid they their hands on them, and they received the Holy Ghost.

Acts 8:14-17

GUIDANCE FOR RECEIVING THE BAPTISM OF THE HOLY SPIRIT AND SPEAKING IN TONGUES

We must understand that a Christian cannot fake to speak in tongues. It is given by the Holy Spirit. If a Christian fakes to speak in tongues, they will be speaking directly to the devil since he is the only deceiver we know in the Bible.

1. **The first qualification for receiving the baptism of the Holy Spirit with the evidence of speaking in tongues is to be born again.**

An unsaved soul cannot therefore receive this gift.

And it came to pass, that, while Apollos was at Corinth, Paul having passed through the upper coasts

came to Ephesus: and finding certain disciples,

He said unto them, Have ye received the Holy Ghost since ye believed?

And he said unto them, Unto what then were ye baptized? And they said, Unto John's baptism.

Then said Paul, John verily baptized with the baptism of repentance, saying unto the people, that they should believe on him which should come after him, that is, on Christ Jesus.

When they heard this, they were baptized in the name of the Lord Jesus.

And when Paul had laid his hands upon them, the Holy Ghost came on them; and they spake with tongues, and prophesied.

Acts 19:1-6

Then Philip went down to the city of Samaria, and preached Christ unto them.

And the people with one accord gave heed unto those things which Philip spake, hearing and seeing the miracles which he did.

For unclean spirits, crying with loud voice, came out of many that were possessed with them: and many taken with palsies, and that were lame, were healed.

And there was great joy in that city.

Acts 8:5-8

Now when the apostles which were at Jerusalem heard that Samaria had received the word of God, they sent unto them Peter and John:

Who, when they were come down, prayed for them, that they might receive the Holy Ghost:

(For as yet he was fallen upon none of them: only they were baptized in the name of the Lord Jesus.)

Then laid they their hands on them, and they received the Holy Ghost.

Acts 8:14-17

2. **Do not beg for the gift because it is a promise from the Lord.**

You should thank God for receiving this free gift. Do not beg for it. I have seen people cry for the gift but their tears does not lead them to receiving the gift. If your friend buys you a birthday gift, do you have to beg for it? No, because they decided to buy you the gift without you asking for it and they will gladly give you the gift. This is exactly what God does. He gladly gives us the gifts He has promised us.

And, being assembled together with them, commanded them that they should not depart from Jerusalem, but wait for the promise of the Father, which, saith he, ye have heard of me.

For John truly baptized with water; but ye shall be baptized with the Holy Ghost not many days hence.

Acts 1:4-5

Then Peter said unto them, Repent, and be baptized every one of you in the name of Jesus Christ for the remission of sins, and ye shall receive the gift of the Holy Ghost.

For the promise is unto you, and to your children, and to all that are afar off, even as many as the Lord our God shall call.

Acts 2:38-39

3. **It is a vocal gift and therefore you must open your mouth and pray.**

Some Christians keep their mouths shut while being prayed for to receive the gift of speaking in tongues. But you should actually be praying in your understanding and at the point of receiving, the Lord will change your tongue by the power of the Holy Ghost. That is why it is called speaking in tongues.

For he that speaketh in an unknown tongue speaketh not unto men, but unto God: for no man understandeth him; howbeit in the spirit he speaketh mysteries.

1 Corinthians 14:2

4. **Do not depend on your mind or what comes into your mind.**

Speaking in tongues is purely the work of the Holy Ghost and therefore your mind is unfruitful. Your mind cannot understand when praying in tongues. If you try to understand what you are speaking, you will say that it does not make sense and you will hinder yourself from receiving. Remember the word of God states that your mind is unfruitful.

For if I pray in an unknown tongue, my spirit prayeth, but my understanding is unfruitful.

1 Corinthians 14:14

5. **Do not think that because of your past sins you cannot receive the gift of speaking in tongues.**

The gift has nothing to do with your past sins. The devil does not want you to receive this gift. He can make you feel that because you have sinned that is why everyone has received the gift except you. But this is simply not true.

Therefore if any man be in Christ, he is a new creature: old things are passed away; behold, all things are become new.

2 Corinthians 5:17

Some people receive the gift suddenly when they are prayed for but for others it can take while. This does not mean that it is because of your sins. Keep on believing God for it and you shall surely receive the gift of speaking in tongues.

6. **Do not think you are going to receive something else or something from the devil. Speaking in tongues is not of the devil, it is a precious gift from the Holy Ghost. It is the Holy Ghost that gives the utterance.**

As I have explained in previous chapters, Jesus Christ is the one who baptises us with the Holy Ghost with the evidence of speaking in tongues, it is not the devil. Have faith to receive it in Jesus name.

I indeed baptize you with water unto repentance: but he that cometh after me is mightier than I, whose shoes I am not worthy to bear: he shall baptize you with the Holy Ghost, and with fire:

Matthew 3:11

And they were all filled with the Holy Ghost, and began to speak with other tongues, as the Spirit gave them utterance.

Acts 2:4

7. **Know that God will definitely give you the gift.**

God is longing to impart you with this gift. He is yearning to let this promise be fulfilled in your life. Open up your heart and receive the gift right now in Jesus name.

If a son shall ask bread of any of you that is a father, will he give him a stone? or if he ask a fish, will he for a fish give him a serpent?

Or if he shall ask an egg, will he offer him a scorpion?

If ye then, being evil, know how to give good gifts unto your children: how much more shall your heavenly Father give the Holy Spirit to them that ask him?

Luke 11:11-13

THE BENEFITS OF SPEAKING IN TONGUES FOR THE BELIEVER

There are many benefits for the believer who speaks in tongues. Desire to speak in tongues and these same benefits will flow to you. Here are just a few of them.

1. You can defeat and overpower the devil.

Jesus said that speaking in tongues is a sign that will follow the believer. Jesus declared that these signs would include casting out devils, taking up serpents and drinking deadly things without harm. These are all signs of the believer's power and authority over the enemy. Jesus also gave speaking in tongues as one of these signs. So therefore, we must yearn and long to speak in tongues in order to overcome the enemy.

And these signs shall follow them that believe; In my name shall they cast out devils; they shall speak with new tongues;

They shall take up serpents; and if they drink any deadly thing, it shall not hurt them; they shall lay hands on the sick, and they shall recover.

Mark 16:17-18

2. The devil does not understand tongues.

Speaking in tongues is such a powerful weapon of warfare because the enemy does not understand it. Whether the enemy is a person or the devil, he cannot understand what is spoken. I often say that when you pray in your understanding, satan understands, and he can make plans to undermine the prayers you have prayed. But when you pray in tongues, he has no clue what is spoken. This is an art of war, use a weapon that your enemy is not aware of.

For he that speaketh in an unknown tongue speaketh not unto men, but unto God: for no man understandeth him; howbeit in the spirit he speaketh mysteries.

1 Corinthians 14:2

3. You build yourself up spiritually.

In 1 Corinthians 14:4, the word of God states that he that speaks in an unknown tongue edifies himself. The word "edify" in this scripture means *"to be a house builder."* This means that when you pray in tongues, you build your spiritual life up and you strengthen and build up your faith.

He that speaketh in an unknown tongue edifieth himself; but he that prophesieth edifieth the church.

1 Corinthians 14:4

In fact, the Bible makes it even clearer in Jude 20, that you build your faith by praying in the Holy Ghost.

But ye, beloved, building up yourselves on your most holy faith, praying in the Holy Ghost,

Jude 20

My faith increases when I speak in tongues and I become charged up like a battery when I speak in tongues. When your phone's battery is getting low, you plug it into a power socket to recharge it. It is the same with the Christian life. Sometimes you can feel very dry but as you speak in tongues, you are fired up again.

4. You pray according to the will of God.

When you pray in tongues, the Holy Spirit gives you utterance. That is, He prays through you and therefore you pray according to the word of God. The Holy Spirit is the author of the word of God and He knows the Bible from Genesis to Revelation. Because He knows the whole word of God, as you pray in tongues, you are automatically praying God's word back to Him without you even realising it. Furthermore, because God's word is His will, you are praying according to the will of God!

When we pray in tongues, the Holy Spirit prays through us using the word of God. The word of God states that we do not know what we should pray for but the Holy Spirit makes intercession for us. The Holy Spirit does this intercession for us by praying through us in the language of the spirit called speaking in tongues. Through this intercession, He the Holy Spirit, enables the body of Christ to pray according to the will of God.

Likewise the Spirit also helpeth our infirmities: for we know not what we should pray for as we ought: but the Spirit itself maketh intercession for us with groanings which cannot be uttered.

And he that searcheth the hearts knoweth what is the mind of the Spirit, because he maketh intercession for the saints according to the will of God.

Romans 8:26-27

5. It helps you to pray for a long time.

I received the Holy Ghost baptism with the evidence of speaking in tongues at the early stages of becoming born again and I can confirm that it has changed my prayer life. The majority of believers have not read the whole Bible nor can they quote the Bible from Genesis to Revelation. So when they pray in their understanding, their prayers mostly last for five minutes. Most Christians find it difficult to wait on God for hours or days because of their inability to pray in tongues. I have spent hours and days in the presence of the Lord and the reason why I am able to spend a long time with the Lord is because I have the gift of speaking in tongues.

Do not misunderstand me. If you know the scriptures very well you can also spend days with God because you will not be praying empty words or praying vain repetitious prayers. I pray both in my understanding and in the spirit but I have realised that when you pray in the spirit you can pray for a long time. You can spend endless hours in prayer to the

Lord because the Holy Spirit prays through you with the word of God.

And he that searcheth the hearts knoweth what is the mind of the Spirit, because he maketh intercession for the saints according to the will of God.

Romans 8:27

6. You become established in the House of the Lord and in the Kingdom of the Lord

When you are imparted with this gift, it causes you to be established and be more committed to the Lord. I have seen people whose Christian lives have transformed dramatically as they received this gift of speaking in tongues.

For I long to see you, that I may impart unto you some spiritual gift, to the end ye may be established;

Romans 1:11

Chapter 8

THE BAPTISM OF FIRE

Many believe God to speak in tongues when being baptised with the Holy Spirit but do not believe God for the baptism of fire. This explains why many tongue speaking Christians continue to wallow in their sins. In Matthew 3:12, the word of God says that Jesus will burn away the chaff with unquenchable fire.

Whose fan is in his hand, and he will throughly purge his floor, and gather his wheat into the garner; but he will burn up the chaff with unquenchable fire.

Matthew 3:12

The fire of God purifies us and purges us. It removes all the unwanted things in our lives and gives us the strength to be holy.

And it shall come to pass, that he that is left in Zion, and he that remaineth in Jerusalem, shall be called holy, even every one that is written among the living in Jerusalem:

When the Lord shall have washed away the filth of the daughters of Zion, and shall have purged the blood of Jerusalem from the midst thereof by the spirit of judgment, and by the spirit of burning.

Isaiah 4:3-4

There is a difference between church members who just receive the baptism of tongues and those who are baptised with fire at the same time. Those who are baptised with fire receive a total transformation and become more conscious of being holy than those who were just baptised with the Holy Spirit with the evidence of speaking in tongues.

Do not just long to speak in tongues but long to receive and to be baptised with the baptism of fire. This is because fire burns, fire consumes and fire destroys the presence of evil. Fire also washes and purifies like soap to make us holy Christians. Receive the fire of the Lord now in the name of Jesus.

Behold, I will send my messenger, and he shall prepare the way before me: and the Lord, whom ye seek, shall suddenly come to his temple, even the messenger of the covenant, whom ye delight in: behold, he shall come, saith the LORD of hosts.

But who may abide the day of his coming? and who shall stand when he appeareth? for he is like a refiner's fire, and like fullers' soap:

And he shall sit as a refiner and purifier of silver: and he shall purify the sons of Levi, and purge them as gold and silver, that they may offer unto the LORD an offering in righteousness.

Malachi 3:1-3

Most lukewarm Christians have not received the fire of the Holy Ghost. This is because fire is hot and it burns. Let's take a look at the signs of a lukewarm believer.

41 SIGNS OF LUKE-WARMNESS

1. Christians who do not dance in church have no fire and are lukewarm.

2. Christians who do not clap their hands during praise and worship have no fire and are lukewarm.

3. Christians who do not receive the word of God with joy have no fire and are lukewarm.

4. Christians who do not say "amen" have no fire and are lukewarm.

5. Christians who do not read their Bible have no fire and are lukewarm.

6. Christians who sleep in church have no fire and are lukewarm.

7. Christians who do not pray have no fire and are lukewarm.

8. Christians who have to be forced to go to church have no fire and are lukewarm.

9. Christians who find themselves at home on Sundays have no fire and are lukewarm.

10. Christians who find themselves at work on Sundays have no fire and are lukewarm.

11. Christians who do not give offerings and pay tithes are bereft of the fire of the Holy Spirit and are lukewarm.

12. Christians who do not know the words of praise and worship songs are dull and devoid of the fire of the Holy Ghost and are lukewarm.

13. Christians who listen to worldly music have no fire and are lukewarm.

14. Christians who have unbeliever friends, boyfriends and girlfriends have no fire and are lukewarm.

15. Christians who only go to church on Sundays and do not go to weekday services have no fire and are lukewarm.

16. Christians who are irregular in going to church have no fire and are lukewarm.

Some Christians go to church this Sunday and do not go to church the following Sunday.

17. Christians who criticise the word of God that has been preached have no fire and are lukewarm.

18. Christians who specialise in criticising pastors have no fire and are lukewarm.

19. Christians who get angry in church and are always quarrelling have no fire and are lukewarm.

20. Christians who are not interested in prayer meetings have no fire and are lukewarm.

21. Christians who remain seated when praise and worship is going on have no fire and are lukewarm.

22. Christians who do not fast have no fire and are lukewarm.

23. Christians who drink alcohol have no fire and are lukewarm.

24. Christians who smoke have no fire and are lukewarm.

25. Christians who dress like prostitutes have no fire and are lukewarm.

You cannot dress like a prostitute to go to church.

You are exposing private parts of your body to everyone. The private parts of a lady belong to her husband and not the general public.

26. Christians who fornicate and commit adultery have no fire and are lukewarm.

A Christian should not be having sex with someone he or she is not married to.

27. Christians who watch pornographic movies have no fire and are lukewarm.

28. Christians who go to nightclubs or discos have no fire and are lukewarm.

29. Christians who go to worldly parties have no fire and are lukewarm.

30. Christians who steal have no fire and are lukewarm.

31. Christians who gossip have no fire and are lukewarm.

32. Christians who cannot quote scriptures have no fire and are lukewarm.

33. Christians who are not straightforward and are full of deceit have no fire and are lukewarm.

34. Christians who are full of worldly proverbs instead of the word of God have no fire and are lukewarm.

35. Christians who are not interested in evangelism or witnessing have no fire and are lukewarm.

36. Christians who are not interested in doing anything in the house of God have no fire and are lukewarm.

A Christian with fire is interested in the work of God. They will join the choir, ushers, welcome team, media team or any working department of the church.

37. Christians who are always late for church services and meetings have no fire and are lukewarm.

38. Christians who do not listen to any praise and worship songs are lukewarm and do not have the fire of the Holy Ghost.

39. Christians who find themselves living together, having sex and producing children and are not married are not on fire and are lukewarm.

I advise such Christians to speak to their pastor to bless their marriage as soon as possible. There is no such thing as a baby father or baby mother in the Bible. It is either a husband or a wife.

40. Christians who are involved in dealing with drugs are devoid of the fire of God and are lukewarm.

41. Christians who receive phone calls, send text messages and browse their phone's internet during church services are lukewarm and are devoid of the fire of God. This is an insult and is disrespectful to the presence of God.

Fire is a sign of life and proves that the believer is alive in Christ Jesus. God does not like lukewarm Christians. He actually told the Christians in the Laodicean church that because they were lukewarm and neither hot nor cold, He will spew them out of His mouth.

This is a warning to Christians who think they can be in the church and play in the world at the same time. God wants us to be hot. If you are not hot then you are cold. Read the passage of scripture below.

And unto the angel of the church of the Laodiceans write;

These things saith the Amen, the faithful and true witness, the beginning of the creation of God;
I know thy works, that thou art neither cold nor hot: I would thou wert cold or hot.

So then because thou art lukewarm, and neither cold nor hot, I will spue thee out of my mouth.

Revelation 3:14-16

Chapter 9

MAINTAINING AND INCREASING YOUR FIRE

As I have mentioned in the previous chapters, when you are filled with the Holy Ghost, you are filled to the brim. But this infilling that comes as a result of the baptism can diminish in terms of quantity, intensity and sharpness if not maintained or increased through certain activities. If you have been a Christian for sometime, you can attest to this fact that there are times that you are so much on fire for the Lord and there were some days that you were so dry and you wondered why this was so. In fact, you can be so dry that you might even think you are not a Christian and that the Lord has left you. But this is not the case. Dryness happens as a result of not maintaining or increasing your fire for the Lord. The good news is that as soon as you begin to perform certain spiritual activities, you are set ablaze again. Being filled with the Holy Spirit is not a one off experience but a continuous and daily experience. We must be filled again and again until it flows out of us to bless others. In other words, we must overflow with the Holy Spirit.

When I was at university, there was a whole week where I could tangibly feel that my spirit, soul and body was full of the Holy Ghost. I could literally feel that I was full of water. This is what I am trying to explain because until we overflow with the Holy Spirit, we can be very dry as Christians. Jesus Himself said that *"out of our belly shall flow rivers of living water."* This is symbolic of being filled with the Holy Spirit until He overflows us.

In the last day, that great day of the feast, Jesus stood and cried, saying,

If any man thirst, let him come unto me, and drink. He that believeth on me, as the scripture hath said, out of his belly shall flow rivers of living water.

(But this spake he of the Spirit, which they that believe on him should receive: for the Holy Ghost was not yet

given; because that Jesus was not yet glorified.)

John 7:37-39

The disciples received the Holy Spirit in John 20:22 when Jesus breathed on them and said to them *"receive ye the Holy Ghost."*

And when he had said this, he breathed on them, and saith unto them, Receive ye the Holy Ghost:

John 20:22

But notice that the disciples did not stop there. They were again filled in Acts 2:4.

And they were all filled with the Holy Ghost, and began to speak with other tongues, as the Spirit gave them utterance.

Acts 2:4

They were filled once more with the Holy Ghost in Acts 4:31.

And when they had prayed, the place was shaken where they were assembled together; and they were all filled with the Holy Ghost, and they spake the word of God with boldness.

Acts 4:31

The disciples were yet again filled in Acts 13:52.

And the disciples were filled with joy, and with the Holy Ghost.

Acts 13:52

God wants to fill us with His Spirit until we want no more. God desires for His children to be filled with His Spirit.

And be not drunk with wine, wherein is excess; but be filled with the Spirit;

Speaking to yourselves in psalms and hymns and spiritual songs, singing and making melody in your heart to the Lord;

Giving thanks always for all things unto God and the Father in the name of our Lord Jesus Christ;

Ephesians 5:18-20

Many are filled with money, wine, alcohol, pride, envy, jealousy, covetousness and the world itself. But the Bible gives us an alternative. Instead of being filled with all these things, we should rather be filled with the Spirit of God. The word "but" in Ephesians 5:18 is translated in the Greek as "alla", which means *"contrariwise, howbeit, indeed, nay, nevertheless, no, notwithstanding, save, therefore, yea, yet."* I like the words "no", "nay", "contrariwise." These words give no room for Christians to be filled with anything else but with the Spirit of God.

The word "filled" is translated "pleroo." In the Greek translation it means *"to level up, to satisfy and to fill up."* Although all born again Christians have a measure of the Spirit of God, the Lord expects all His children to be filled and be full of the Holy Spirit.

Dear Lord Jesus,
Please baptise me with the
Holy Ghost and with fire.
Please help me to maintain
my fire for You.
Keep me ablaze for You all the days of my
life, in the name of Jesus.
Burn every form of luke-warmness from
my life, in the name of Jesus.
Lord help me to be on fire all the days of
my life, in the name of Jesus.

Chapter 10

SPIRITUAL ACTIVITIES THAT MAINTAIN AND INCREASE YOUR FIRE FOR THE LORD

Worship

Learn how to worship the Lord alone in your room. I have come to realise that worship brings down the presence of God faster than prayer. Do not get me wrong because I believe in prayer, but worship is the fastest way to rekindle your fire for the Lord. Sometimes I worship the Lord for more than an hour before I start praying and I experience an immense presence of the Lord. Worship automatically rekindles and increases your fire for the Lord. Intentionally learn worship songs, learn the words and sing them to the Lord. If you do not know the words, play anointed worship songs and sing along.

Enter into his gates with thanksgiving, and into his courts with praise: be thankful unto him, and bless his name.

Psalm 100:4

Prayer

Every believer must each learn how to spend time with the Lord in prayer. A lack of prayer in a Christian's life makes that Christian very dry and fleshy. After I have spent time in prayer with the Lord, I leave His presence charged and on fire. We must learn to be alone with the Lord in prayer in order to maintain and increase our fire for the Lord.

Even the youths shall faint and be weary, and the young men shall utterly fall:

But they that wait upon the LORD shall renew their strength; they shall mount up with wings as eagles; they shall run, and not be weary; and they shall walk, and not faint.

Isaiah 40:30-31

The Word of God

Your love for the word of God will also increase your fire for the Lord. Read your Bible daily and believe what you read. Ask the Holy Spirit for revelations and as you receive these revelations, it will rekindle your fire for the Lord. Our God is a consuming fire and the word of God is God.

For our God is a consuming fire.

Hebrews 12:29

In the beginning was the Word, and the Word was with God, and the Word was God.

John 1:1

If the word of God is God Himself and the word is a consuming fire, it means it has the ability to set you on fire as you read it.

Listening to Anointed Preaching Messages and Watching Preaching Videos

I listen to preaching messages every day and I watch preaching videos all the time. I do not just listen to anyone but I listen and soak in my spiritual father's messages and other anointed men of God's messages.

Jesus said that his spoken words are spirit and life.

It is the spirit that quickeneth; the flesh profiteth nothing: the words that I speak unto you, they are spirit, and they are life.

John 6:63

So as you listen and watch, the spirit and the life of the word of God is imparted to us and sets us on fire. Ezekiel said that *"the spirit entered into me when he spake unto me."*

And he said unto me, Son of man, stand upon thy feet, and I will speak unto thee.

And the spirit entered into me when he spake unto me, and set me upon my feet, that I heard him that spake unto me.

Ezekiel 2:1-2

Reading Anointed Christian Books

Do not underestimate the power of a Christian book. A book has the power to change your life especially when it has been written by an anointed preacher. But be careful what you read because many have written Christian books just to make money. You can often tell when reading these books because there is no anointing that sets you on fire. Spend money to buy books and read them expecting God to touch you through the book. I read a lot, so much in fact that I almost have a bookshop in my house.

I remember one day, I was feeling spiritually dry and I took Rev. Kenneth Hagin's book, "I Believe in Visions" and immediately my fire was rekindled and I was set ablaze for Jesus. Apostle Paul, who wrote almost half of the New Testament, was a zealous reader.

The cloke that I left at Troas with Carpus, when thou comest, bring with thee, and the books, but especially the parchments.

2 Timothy 4:13

The angel of the Lord also commanded Apostle John to take the little book and eat it.

And the voice which I heard from heaven spake unto me again, and said, Go and take the little book which is open in the hand of the angel which standeth upon the sea and upon the earth.

And I went unto the angel, and said unto him, Give me the little book. And he said unto me, Take it, and eat it

up; and it shall make thy belly bitter, but it shall be in thy mouth sweet as honey.

Revelation 10:8-9

Soul Winning or Evangelism

There is a certain joy that mothers experience when they give birth. This joy makes them forget the pain they went through to bring forth that precious baby. This joy and excitement is similar to that which we experience when we obey the Lord to evangelise the lost for Him.

A woman when she is in travail hath sorrow, because her hour is come: but as soon as she is delivered of the child, she remembereth no more the anguish, for joy that a man is born into the world.

John 16:21

Even the times you go for evangelism and you don't win a soul, there is still a certain joy you experience by just talking to people about Jesus. I am talking about this joy because it energises and rekindles our fire for the Lord.

Soul winning is the heart beat of God. It is for this very reason that Jesus was crucified on the Cross for our sins.

I say unto you, that likewise joy shall be in heaven over one sinner that repenteth, more than over ninety and nine just persons, which need no repentance.

Luke 15:7

Hunger and Thirst

Being hungry and thirsty for the Lord provokes the Lord to fill us with the Holy Spirit. We must be hungry for the things of God. You should be hungry to go to church, you should be hungry for His word and you should be hungry to be in His presence. When the Lord realises that He is all you want, He will rush to fill you up. Hunger and thirst go hand in hand because when you are hungry, you thirst for what you are hungry for. We are often hungry and thirsty for food and natural water but God wants us to be hungry and thirsty for the Holy Spirit. Elizabeth declared that God has filled the hungry.

He hath filled the hungry with good things; and the rich he hath sent empty away.

Luke 1:53

Any time I am holding a church meeting, I look at the face of those who are hungry for Jesus. These group of people often have strong faith to receive as a result of their hunger and they are always touched by the Lord. Meanwhile, others sit in the church like dead wood expecting the pastor to wind them up and set them on fire. The second often leave the service not touched at all. This is why Jesus said that those who are hungry and thirsty shall be filled.

Blessed are they which do hunger and thirst after righteousness: for they shall be filled.

Matthew 5:6

Jesus also said all those who are thirsty should come unto him and He will fill them until the river flows out of them.

In the last day, that great day of the feast, Jesus stood and cried, saying, If any man thirst, let him come unto me, and drink.

He that believeth on me, as the scripture hath said, out of his belly shall flow rivers of living water.

(But this spake he of the Spirit, which they that believe on him should receive: for the Holy Ghost was not yet given; because that Jesus was not yet glorified.)

John 7:37-39

This is the most important point for being filled again and again with the Holy Spirit. Your hunger and thirst is what causes you to worship, pray, read the Bible, listen to preaching messages and watch preaching videos, read Christian books and go for evangelism.

Father in the name of Jesus,
I ask You to enable me to experience
the reality and
power of the Holy Spirit.
You said these signs shall follow
those who believe.
In Your name O Lord, use me to cast out devils, raise the dead, heal the sick and preach the gospel.
Lord, let sign and wonders manifest in my life and ministry by the manifestation of the Holy Spirit in my life.
In Jesus mighty name, Amen.

Chapter 11

THE REALITY AND THE POWER OF THE HOLY SPIRIT

The Holy Spirit is the power of the Godhead and His power is beyond any other power on this earth. It was the power of the Holy Spirit that created the earth and turned that which was chaos into the beautiful earth that we see today.

And the earth was without form, and void; and darkness was upon the face of the deep. And the Spirit of God moved upon the face of the waters.

Genesis 1:2

The Spirit of God moved and the Lord said *"let there be"* and there was. Remember the void and the chaos was quickly transformed by the power of the Holy Ghost. The Holy Spirit makes the manifestations of the Lord real to us and transports what is in the spiritual realm to us in the physical realm. He makes the invisible visible to us.

Power to Heal

The word of God tells us that it was the power of the Holy Spirit that enabled Jesus to heal the sick and to do good. Without the Holy Spirit, Jesus was not able to heal the sick.

How God anointed Jesus of Nazareth with the Holy Ghost and with power: who went about doing good, and healing all that were oppressed of the devil; for God was with him.

Acts 10:38

The Holy Spirit causes healing to take place in our bodies. Through the power of the Holy Spirit, there is no sickness on earth that God cannot heal.

And Jesus went about all Galilee, teaching in their synagogues, and preaching the gospel of the kingdom,

and healing all manner of sickness and all manner of disease among the people.

Matthew 4:23

In His presence, sicknesses and diseases disappear, sicknesses melt and die. I have seen cancers disappear from the bodies of God's children and diverse forms of diseases and sicknesses healed. The body of Christ must believe in healing and walk in divine health. Healing belongs to us and it is the fruit of salvation. The Lord does not want His children to be sick because sickness comes from the pit of hell and it must be rejected. It is illegal in our bodies.

Power to Raise the Dead and to Give Life

Jesus raised the dead by the power of the Holy Spirit. Even Jesus Himself was raised from the dead by the power of the Holy Spirit.

But if the Spirit of him that raised up Jesus from the dead dwell in you, he that raised up Christ from the dead shall also quicken your mortal bodies by his Spirit that dwelleth in you.

Romans 8:11

Therefore, if the Holy Spirit had refused to raise Jesus from the dead, He would still be in the grave. It was the power of the Holy Spirit that gave our Lord Jesus victory over the grave. The grave could not hold Him, it could not overcome Him. He defeated the grave for our sakes by the power of the Holy Spirit. When Jesus told Lazarus come forth, suddenly the Holy Spirit revived his dead body and brought his spirit back into him and he lived again. Lazarus was dead for four days and stinking but the power of the Holy Spirit knows no limit. It does not know anything like death because there is life whenever He comes on the scene.

And when he thus had spoken, he cried with a loud voice, Lazarus, come forth.

And he that was dead came forth, bound hand and foot with graveclothes: and his face was bound about with a napkin. Jesus saith unto them, Loose him, and let him go.

John 11:43-44

The Holy Spirit indeed is the life giver. God formed man from the dust of the earth but man was not alive. He was in a dead state without any sign of life. Then suddenly, God breathed into man His blessed Holy Spirit who is the breath of life, and man became a living soul.

And the LORD God formed man of the dust of the ground, and breathed into his nostrils the breath of life; and man became a living soul.

Genesis 2:7

The Spirit of God hath made me, and the breath of the Almighty hath given me life.

Job 33:4

Power to Save and to Transform

It is the Holy Spirit that causes salvation to take place. He has a convicting power that is able to save the most hardcore sinner and transform them into a saint. Change only comes from the Holy Spirit.

Our society is breeding more and more young people who cannot be controlled by laws, rules and regulations of the land. Yet these same young people, who outsmart the police and cannot be helped by the social services, can be transformed and tamed by the power of the Holy Spirit. He can turn them into anointed men and women of God. The power of the Holy Spirit will change young men and women and make them responsible people in society who are not interested in filling the land with violence.

And when he is come, he will reprove the world of sin, and of righteousness, and of judgment:

John 16:8

Power to Free from Bondage

Now the Lord is that Spirit: and where the Spirit of the Lord is, there is liberty.

2 Corinthians 3:17

I love this verse. There is freedom in the presence of God. There is no bondage there because we have not received a spirit of bondage again to fear but the Spirit of God. The Holy Spirit will free you from sin, poverty, sicknesses and diseases. He will set you free from the power of alcohol and drug addiction. He will set you free from addiction to pornography and evil desires. Above all, He is able to break every chain that binds you and the burdens you carry.

And it shall come to pass in that day, that his burden shall be taken away from off thy shoulder, and his yoke from off thy neck, and the yoke shall be destroyed because of the anointing.

Isaiah 10:27

Signs, Wonders and Miracles

And by the hands of the apostles were many signs and wonders wrought among the people; (and they were all with one accord in Solomon's porch.

Acts 5:12

The Holy Spirit causes signs and wonders to happen which are beyond human imagination and comprehension. Jesus walked on water and calmed the storm by the power of the Holy Spirt.

And in the fourth watch of the night Jesus went unto them, walking on the sea.

Matthew 14:25

And when they had sent away the multitude, they took him even as he was in the ship. And there were also with him other little ships.

And there arose a great storm of wind, and the waves beat into the ship, so that it was now full.

And he was in the hinder part of the ship, asleep on a pillow: and they awake him, and say unto him, Master, carest thou not that we perish?

And he arose, and rebuked the wind, and said unto the sea, Peace, be still. And the wind ceased, and there was a great calm.

Mark 4:36-39

It was through the power of the Holy Spirit that Jesus turned water into wine at the wedding in Cana. Just think about it. How can water become wine instantly? It is only through the touch of the blessed Holy Spirit.

And the third day there was a marriage in Cana of Galilee; and the mother of Jesus was there:

And both Jesus was called, and his disciples, to the marriage.

And when they wanted wine, the mother of Jesus saith unto him, They have no wine.

Jesus saith unto her, Woman, what have I to do with thee? mine hour is not yet come.

His mother saith unto the servants, Whatsoever he saith unto you, do it.

And there were set there six waterpots of stone, after

the manner of the purifying of the Jews, containing two or three firkins apiece.

Jesus saith unto them, Fill the waterpots with water. And they filled them up to the brim.

And he saith unto them, Draw out now, and bear unto the governor of the feast. And they bare it.

When the ruler of the feast had tasted the water that was made wine, and knew not whence it was: (but the servants which drew the water knew;) the governor of the feast called the bridegroom,

And saith unto him, Every man at the beginning doth set forth good wine; and when men have well drunk, then that which is worse: but thou hast kept the good wine until now.

This beginning of miracles did Jesus in Cana of Galilee, and manifested forth his glory; and his disciples believed on him.

John 2:1-11

Casting out Devils

Do you realise that without the Holy Spirit, Jesus

could not cast out devils? It is the power of the Holy Spirit that causes demons to tremble and to flee. The same Holy Spirit manifested Himself through the Lord Jesus to cast out devils. The Pharisees could not understand this and thought that Jesus casted out devils using the spirit of satan. But Jesus made it known to them that He was able to cast out devils by the power of the Holy Spirit.

But when the Pharisees heard it, they said, This fellow doth not cast out devils, but by Beelzebub the prince of the devils.

And Jesus knew their thoughts, and said unto them, Every kingdom divided against itself is brought to desolation; and every city or house divided against itself shall not stand:

And if Satan cast out Satan, he is divided against himself; how shall then his kingdom stand?
And if I by Beelzebub cast out devils, by whom do your children cast them out? therefore they shall be your judges.

But if I cast out devils by the Spirit of God, then the kingdom of God is come unto you.

Matthew 12:24-28

Chapter 12

PHYSICAL MANIFESTATIONS OF THE HOLY SPIRIT

The Holy Spirit has a way of expressing and demonstrating Himself to the saints. When he comes on the scene, He makes Himself visible so that all can see. The word "manifestation" in 1 Corinthians 12:7 means *"demonstration, sign, appearance, expression, materialization and symptom."*

But the manifestation of the Spirit is given to every man to profit withal.

1 Corinthians 12:7

These demonstrations in themselves are not for a show to the saints but they are spiritual encounters purposed to change the life of the believer. However, unbelievers and many so called Christians blaspheme against these appearances of the Holy Ghost thinking that it is some kind of evil spirit manifesting through the people of God.

One day while ministering, and as the presence of God was moving mightily in the congregation, a lady and a gentleman ran out of the church fearing for their lives. On another occasion while I was ministering and praying for people, a gentleman who I knew was not saved, ran out of the church whenever the Spirit of God started moving. On both occasions, when I questioned these people after the service, they all had the same answer. They were terrified by His presence. This is exactly what happened to the people who were with Daniel.

And I Daniel alone saw the vision: for the men that were with me saw not the vision; but a great quaking fell upon them, so that they fled to hide themselves.

Daniel 10:7

But we as Christians must love His presence and His moves in our midst. We must acquaint ourselves with His physical manifestations and demonstrations in the life of the believer. Since I became a Christian, I have experienced several demonstrations and manifestations of the Holy Ghost and I have also witnessed them in other people's lives as well. Below are some of the physical manifestations of the Holy Spirit, along with scriptures.

Trembling, Shaking or Quaking

The presence of the Holy Spirit causes people to tremble or shake uncontrollably. Sometimes the person is being touched in a special way and at other times an evil spirit is leaving a person as a result of the presence of the Lord. Whichever be the case, the end result is to deposit the goodness of the Lord in that person. Shaking, quaking and trembling are all similar experiences that takes place when the Holy Spirit manifests Himself in the lives of God's people.

Fear ye not me? saith the LORD: will ye not tremble at my presence, which have placed the sand for the bound of the sea by a perpetual decree, that it cannot pass it: and though the waves thereof toss themselves, yet can they not prevail; though they roar, yet can they not pass over it?

Jeremiah 5:22

Tremble, thou earth, at the presence of the Lord, at the presence of the God of Jacob;

Psalm 114:7

The LORD reigneth; let the people tremble:

he sitteth between the cherubims; let the earth be moved.

Psalm 99:1

And I Daniel alone saw the vision: for the men that were with me saw not the vision; but a great quaking fell upon them, so that they fled to hide themselves.

Daniel 10:7

Mine heart within me is broken because of the prophets; all my bones shake; I am like a drunken man, and like a man whom wine hath overcome, because of the LORD, and because of the words of his holiness.

Jeremiah 23:9

Falling Down

There are several scriptures in the Bible about people falling down when they came into contact with the presence of the Lord. I have fallen down several times under the presence of the Holy Spirit and I have also witnessed others falling. You can have a spectacular encounter with the Lord through falling under His presence.

One Sunday morning during service, a Muslim lady who was visiting the church for the first time, fell from her chair while sitting down. She fell under the power of God and began to shake, tremble and scream uncontrollably. I had never seen that before because I thought these experiences happened to only Christians. Yet before my very eyes, here was a Muslim, who was not saved and she was having an encounter with the Lord right in the midst of the congregation. When she came back to herself, she said that while the ministration was going on, she suddenly saw herself going down through a dark tunnel which according to her was hell.

In her own words, she said she saw herself going to hell. She said she tried to come out but a certain force was pulling her down and she felt her body eating away. As she was screaming for help, she suddenly saw a bright light which I believe is a reflection of Jesus Christ of Nazareth. As soon as she saw the bright light, she saw herself floating out of the tunnel towards the light. She gave her testimony and told the whole congregation that she now realised that Christians and Muslims do not serve the same God. Halleluyah! Amen. This lady is now a born again Christian and she is serving the Lord.

Through falling down, this lady's life was transformed just like Apostle Paul's in Acts chapter 9.

And as he journeyed, he came near Damascus: and suddenly there shined round about him a light from heaven: And he fell to the earth, and heard a voice saying unto him, Saul, Saul, why persecutest thou me?

Acts 9:3-4

And when the ass saw the angel of the LORD, she fell down under Balaam: and Balaam's anger was kindled, and he smote the ass with a staff.

Numbers 22:27

It came even to pass, as the trumpeters and singers were as one, to make one sound to be heard in praising and thanking the LORD; and when they lifted up their voice with the trumpets and cymbals and instruments of musick, and praised the LORD, saying, For he is good; for his mercy endureth for ever: that then the house was filled with a cloud, even the house of the LORD;

So that the priests could not stand to minister by reason of the cloud: for the glory of the LORD had filled the house of God.

2 Chronicles 5:13-14

While he yet spake, behold, a bright cloud overshadowed them: and behold a voice out of the cloud, which said, This is my beloved Son, in whom I am well pleased; hear ye him.

And when the disciples heard it, they fell on their face, and were sore afraid.

Matthew 17:5-6

They answered him, Jesus of Nazareth. Jesus saith unto them, I am he. And Judas also, which betrayed him, stood with them.

As soon then as he had said unto them, I am he, they went backward, and fell to the ground.

John 18:5-6

Drunkenness

Sometimes people behave as if they are drunk when they encounter the Holy Spirit. In the natural, when a person is drunk he or she begins to exhibit certain behaviours. The behaviour of a person who is drunk in the Spirit is similar to someone who is drunk naturally except that the one drunk in the Spirit does not misbehave. That is why the word of God states that do not be drunk with wine but be drunk with the Spirit.

And be not drunk with wine, wherein is excess; but be filled with the Spirit;

Ephesians 5:18

Mine heart within me is broken because of the prophets; all my bones shake; I am like a drunken man, and like a man whom wine hath overcome, because of the LORD, and because of the words of his holiness.

Jeremiah 23:9

For these are not drunken, as ye suppose, seeing it is but the third hour of the day.

But this is that which was spoken by the prophet Joel;

And it shall come to pass in the last days, saith God, I will pour out of my Spirit upon all flesh: and your sons and your daughters shall prophesy, and your young men shall see visions, and your old men shall dream dreams:

And on my servants and on my handmaidens I will pour out in those days of my Spirit; and they shall prophesy:

And I will shew wonders in heaven above, and signs in the earth beneath; blood, and fire, and vapour of smoke:

Acts 2:15-19

Joy and Laughter

Sometimes people come to church very depressed with many kind of problems. As a result of the issues in their lives, they have no joy and their faces are always gloomy and they do not laugh at anything. But when these same people encounter the Holy Spirit, the Lord is able to cause them to laugh and be joyful. After such an encounter, the spirit of depression and heaviness is removed and replaced with joy and laughter.

I command the spirit of depression and heaviness to leave you right now in Jesus name. Receive the spirit of joy and laughter and may the Lord fill your life with happiness.

To appoint unto them that mourn in Zion, to give unto them beauty for ashes, the oil of joy for mourning, the garment of praise for the spirit of heaviness; that they might be called trees of righteousness, the planting of the LORD, that he might be glorified.

Isaiah 61:3

When the LORD turned again the captivity of Zion, we were like them that dream.

Then was our mouth filled with laughter and our tongue with singing: then said they among the heathen,

The LORD hath done great things for them.

The LORD hath done great things for us; whereof we are glad.

Turn again our captivity, O LORD, as the streams in the south.
They that sow in tears shall reap in joy.

He that goeth forth and weepeth, bearing precious seed, shall doubtless come again with rejoicing, bringing his sheaves with him.

Psalm 126:1-6

Then he said unto them, Go your way, eat the fat, and drink the sweet, and send portions unto them for whom nothing is prepared: for this day is holy unto our Lord: neither be ye sorry; for the joy of the LORD is your strength.

Nehemiah 8:10

Make a joyful noise unto the LORD, all ye lands.

Serve the LORD with gladness: come before his presence with singing.

Know ye that the LORD he is God: it is he that hath

made us, and not we ourselves; we are his people, and the sheep of his pasture.

Enter into his gates with thanksgiving, and into his courts with praise: be thankful unto him, and bless his name.

For the LORD is good; his mercy is everlasting; and his truth endureth to all generations.

Psalm 100:1-5

Then shall the virgin rejoice in the dance, both young men and old together: for I will turn their mourning into joy, and will comfort them, and make them rejoice from their sorrow.

Jeremiah 31:13

Running Under the Presence of God

I was in a service one day while on the university campus when the man of God said that the apostolic anointing is coming upon someone. Suddenly the Spirit of God came upon me and I began to run around in the congregation. It was the same presence of God that caused Prophet Elijah to run and overtake Ahab.

And it came to pass in the mean while, that the heaven was black with clouds and wind, and there was a great rain.

And Ahab rode, and went to Jezreel. And the hand of the LORD was on Elijah; and he girded up his loins, and ran before Ahab to the entrance of Jezreel.

1 Kings 18:45-46

Weeping

Sometimes people weep under the presence of God when they are overwhelmed by His presence. At other times, people weep as they are convicted by the Holy Spirit.

Because thine heart was tender, and thou didst humble thyself before God, when thou heardest his words against this place, and against the inhabitants thereof, and humbledst thyself before me, and didst rend thy clothes, and weep before me; I have even heard thee also, saith the LORD.

2 Chronicles 34:27

Yea, he had power over the angel, and prevailed: he wept, and made supplication unto him: he found him in Bethel, and there he spake with us;

Hosea 12:4

And Peter remembered the word of Jesus, which said unto him, Before the cock crow, thou shalt deny me thrice. And he went out, and wept bitterly.

Matthew 26:75

And I wept much, because no man was found worthy to open and to read the book, neither to look thereon.

Revelation 5:4

Who in the days of his flesh, when he had offered up prayers and supplications with strong crying and tears unto him that was able to save him from death, and was heard in that he feared;

Hebrews 5:7

Heat

I was praying for a lady with cancer one day, and she told me that whilst my hand was on her head, she felt heat passing through her body. This lady was healed instantly under such a strong presence of God. I mentioned earlier that the Holy Spirit is likened to fire. You and I know that where there is fire there is heat. Naturally, three things are needed to start fire; oxygen, fuel and heat. So where there is fire, heat is always present.

For so the LORD said unto me, I will take my rest, and I will consider in my dwelling place like a clear heat upon herbs, and like a cloud of dew in the heat of harvest.

Isaiah 18:4

So the spirit lifted me up, and took me away, and I went in bitterness, in the heat of my spirit; but the hand of the LORD was strong upon me.

Ezekiel 3:14

Chapter 13

PRACTICAL MANIFESTATIONS OF THE HOLY SPIRIT IN MY LIFE AND MINISTRY

As I mentioned, I am now a full-time minister, preaching, teaching and healing under the anointing of the Holy Spirit of God. I noticed the call of God very early when I became born again Christian in the year 2000. The dreams and the visions the Holy Spirit gave me were the signs of the call of God on my life. These began to manifest physically in my life as I ministered as a student elder. As a student, I entered into services and more meetings with the power and presence of the Holy Spirit all over me. There was a strong manifestation of the Holy Spirit and His power during my meetings. It became so strong that I was nicknamed Holy Ghost Elder. Since my encounter with the Holy Spirit, He has never left me and is always with me. Even till this day I see the anointing on my life waxing stronger and stronger.

Two weeks before I started my church Living Jesus Tabernacle, I had another encounter with the Holy Spirit during which I received the baptism of fire. I attended Night of Wonders service at Victorious Pentecostal Church also known as VPA. The founder is Pastor Alex Omokudu and he was the one ministering that night. Pastor Alex is a great man of God with a heavy anointing for signs and wonders. While he was ministering, he called me out of the large crowd that had gathered in the auditorium that night. Out of the blue, he said "young man come here, either you are a minister or you are now going to start a church and you need the fire of God to start a church." As he spoke, he suddenly laid his hands on me and I felt fire go through my entire body. I laid on the floor and shook for a long time. This happened around 4am in the early morning of April 6th 2013.

On the night of April 13th 2013, something else happened. The Lord gave me a dream confirming that He had called me to do His work. In the dream, the Lord gave me this scripture; 1 Peter 2:4. This was a confirmation of the call to remove any form of doubt that the voice of people might create.

To whom coming, as unto a living stone, disallowed indeed of men, but chosen of God, and precious,

1 Peter 2:4

After this encounter, I have seen many signs and wonders in my life and ministry and I will share some with you. I never ever try to put the Holy Spirit in a box. I allow Him to move and minister to His people once He shows up during our meetings.

Disappearance of a Lump

A lady had a lump in her body and had seen the doctor several times. During one of our programs called Healing in His Wings, the lump disappeared from her body by the touch of the Holy Spirit. Because of where the lump was located on her body, she did not even realise that she no longer had the lump. It was in the morning whilst bathing that she noticed that the lump was no longer there. She and her husband testified about the goodness of the Lord.

Bursting of a Cist

I once visited a couple at home and when I was about to leave, I asked them what they wanted the Lord to do for them. The husband did not say anything but the wife started crying so I asked why. According to the wife, she had a cist on her back. She had already undergone surgery and it was cut off but it had started growing again and the doctor had scheduled to perform another surgery in four weeks time. I asked if she believed that God could heal her and she responded with a resounding yes. I laid my hands on her and commanded the cist to wither and she fell under the power as the presence of the Lord was present. I left their home and told her that she would have a dream in the night.

According to the wife, in the night while she was sleeping she had a dream in which she saw that the cist had burst. When she woke up, she realised that it was not just a dream but a reality. The power of the Lord had caused the cist to burst and wither. The lady went to see the doctor and the doctor said she no longer needed any surgery to be performed. I thank God for His healing power.

Disappearance of Fibroid

A lady discovered she had a fibroid situated at the mouth of the womb. Because of that, the doctors decided to perform surgery to remove the fibroid along with her womb. She was devastated at hearing such news. This lady decided to attend one of our programs called Break Every Chain. I called her to the front and asked her to lay down in front of the congregation. I anointed her with oil and commanded the fibroid to disappear. The day of the surgery came and when the surgeons rechecked the womb, the fibroid had disappeared. Glory be to God! As I write this book, this lady is now happily married with her womb intact and fibroid free. God healed her through the power of the Holy Ghost.

A Man Delivered from Drug Addiction

A man who was addicted to drugs and was going mental was miraculously delivered by the power of God during our Holy Ghost Fire conference. He encountered the Holy Spirit during the service and gave his life to Jesus. He is no longer on drugs to the glory of God.

A Young Lady Delivered from Drug Addiction and Madness

A young lady who was heavily addicted to hardcore drugs and had no hope or aspirations was miraculously delivered by the power of God. All this lady knew was to smoke cocaine and other hard drugs and sleep. According to her own words, she said that the drugs had affected her mind. She did not want to work or doing anything in this life. But by the grace and power of God, this lady is saved, delivered from drugs and she is now a Holy Ghost filled, tongues speaking Christian. She also now has a job and is earning good money. Glory be to God in the highest!

A Lady Healed Miraculously

I was at home one day when my wife called to ask if I could go and pray for one of her customers. She had not seen this customer for a long time and when she saw her, she had lost a lot of weight. So she asked her what had happened and the customer said she had not been able to use the toilet for two years. She had undergone several operations but she had still not been able to go to toilet. As soon as my wife told me this, I recognised the activities of witchcraft in this lady's life so I agreed to go and pray for her. When we visited the lady's house, she told me she wanted to go back to her home country in Africa. I told her not to, because if she did, she would be buying her own coffin. While praying with my hands on her, I felt as though the Lord was saying the toilet was coming out so I asked her to go to the toilet immediately. When she went, nothing came out. I left her house and said to her that she was going to have a visitation that night.

She called in the morning to say that she had now been able to go to toilet freely without any struggle. So I asked what happened that night. According to her own words, in the night while she was sleeping, she felt a hand touch her from her head to her feet. She immediately knew the Lord had sent His angel to touch her. When she woke up in the morning, she was totally healed and she was able to go to toilet. Glory be to Jesus!

A Muslim Lady's Supernatural Encounter with the Lord in Church

A Muslim visited our church one Sunday morning and while the ministration was going on, she fell under the power of God. This was an amazing sight to watch because this was an unbeliever who has fallen under the power of God. She was banging her hands on the floor, screaming and shaking uncontrollably. Even the ushers could not control her. When she finally came to herself, she started weeping. I asked her what happened to her when she was on the floor and she began to speak.

According to her, while she was sitting in the service, she saw a bright light and fell to the floor. While on the floor, she saw herself going down through a dark tunnel. She said she felt like her body was being eaten away and a force was pulling her into the dark which she described as Hell. According to her, as this was happening she started screaming for help, but the more she screamed, the more she went down. But as she kept on screaming for help, she suddenly saw a light which was so bright that she could not look on it. She began floating towards this light and she felt so peaceful. This Muslim lady said to the whole congregation that she now realises that Christians and Muslims do not serve the same God. I asked her if she wanted to give her life to Jesus and without hesitation, she said yes. I led her to say the sinner's prayer and she is a Christian till this day. May the name of the Lord be praised!

Supernatural Pregnancy of a Lady

I was told of a couple who were going through so much difficulty in trying to conceive a child. The lady first conceived and the child died in the womb, she conceived again and the baby died once again. When I was told by this couple's friend, I sensed that there was witchcraft involvement so I asked their friend to request that they attend our Break Every Chain program. The husband could not attend but the wife came. During the ministration, I was instructed by the Lord to give her my suit jacket to wear for her total deliverance. She fell under the power of the Holy Spirit and she was instantly delivered. The Lord asked me to tell her to sleep with the husband that very night and that she was going to conceive and this one will remain to full-term and be delivered. The lady obeyed and did as the Lord instructed.

Her deliverance took place on a Friday, she committed love with her husband that Friday night and by the following Wednesday, I had a phone call from the husband rejoicing that the wife was pregnant. A beautiful baby was safely born nine months later. Glory be to Jesus in the highest!

A Man Miraculously Passed His Practical Driving Test

A man who had always been a very good driver had a fatal car accident which caused him to be imprisoned. His driving license was also revoked due to the seriousness of the incident. Upon release from prison, he started trying to get his license back but it was an uphill battle. He undertook the practical driving test six times over a number of years and each time he failed.

Although he had proved he could drive, they still failed him. This was because no one wanted to give him a license as they perceived it could happen again. But during our Break Every Chain program, the Lord asked me to instruct him to go and rebook his driving test and that He the Lord would give him an examiner who will pass him. This gentleman obeyed, booked his driving test and he passed. According to him, when the examiner said he had passed, he thought the examiner said he had failed. He could not believe what he was hearing. The Lord had passed him as He said. Glory be to His name!

Disappearance of Pain

A lady came to church limping on the right leg during our Holy Ghost Fire conference. I laid my hands on her the pain left immediately. She was instantly healed by the power of the Holy Ghost. Glory be to Jesus! Two ladies came to church one Sunday morning with extreme pain in their right legs and the power of God healed them instantly. The pain left as I laid my hands on them.

This and many more miracles has the Holy Spirit performed in my life and ministry. I have seen Him do so much in my life and ministry and He is about to do the same for you if you would allow Him into your life. He is longing to have a relationship with you and to be your friend. If you will invite him into your life, He will transform you into an anointed vessel for the Lord.

If there is any sickness in your body say this prayer after me:

Father in the name of Jesus, I come against every sickness in my body. I command every sickness in my body to wither and die by the power of the Holy Ghost.

Holy Spirit, flow through my body right now form the crown of my head to the soles of my feet and remove anything in my body that is not of God in the name of Jesus.

I command the spirit of depression to leave me right now and I declare my mind free from demonic oppression in the name of Jesus.

Lord Jesus, by your stripes I am healed and I walk in divine health. No sickness will come to my body again because you have healed me. Thank you for your healing power in Jesus name.

Father in the name of Jesus,
I pray that the gifts of healing, word of wisdom, word of knowledge,
faith, gifts of prophecy, working of miracles, discerning spirit,
tongues and interpretation of tongues begin to manifest in my life.
May I experience these gifts in my life and ministry in the name of Jesus.

Chapter 14

GIFTS OF THE SPIRIT

This chapter is to introduce you to the gifts of the Spirit that are available to us as Christians and to encourage you to earnestly covet these gifts as stated in the word of God. It amazes me that you see Christians asking God for husbands, wives, cars, houses, new jobs, good education and good health but fail to ask for spiritual gifts. You can ask the Lord for spiritual gifts as well because we need these gifts to function effectively as Christians.

That is why the word of God encourages us not to be ignorant of them.

Now concerning spiritual gifts, brethren, I would not have you ignorant.

1 Corinthians 12:1

These gifts are not for Apostles, Prophets, Evangelists, Pastors and Teachers only. They are for all believers or ordinary Christians as well. All God's children are entitled to the gifts of the Spirit, not just a selected few. Many have not longed to have these gifts because they think that they are only for those called to the ministry. But it is not so. It is for all believers as the scripture says.

But the manifestation of the Spirit is given to every man to profit withal.

1 Corinthians 12:7

There are profits associated to these gifts and we must long and yearn to be imparted with them. When I became born again, I asked the Lord for all these gifts. The Lord can decide to give one person all the nine gifts and therefore I coveted earnestly for all the gifts. Over the years I have seen these gifts operated through my ministry as the Spirit wills.

The gifts of the Spirit are different from the Offices of the Ministry. One can have the gift of prophecy but it does not mean that the person is a Prophet or standing in the office of the Prophet. The Offices of the Ministry are Apostles, Prophets, Evangelists, Pastors and Teachers. These are special callings that the Lord calls His people to function in the ministry.

And he gave some, apostles; and some, prophets; and some, evangelists; and some, pastors and teachers;

Ephesians 4:11

So do not start giving yourself titles as the gifts of the Spirit start to manifest in you. There are so many people calling themselves prophets nowadays just because they prophesied one or two times. First of all, you cannot force these gifts to work through you. You cannot let the gift operate any time you want it to operate. The Holy Spirit Himself allows these gifts to operate through you, when He chooses, in order to fulfil His purpose. Do not fake the gifts as you will only be deceiving yourself and others.

Whoso boasteth himself of a false gift is like clouds and wind without rain.

Proverbs 25:14

There are nine gifts of the Spirit listed in the Bible and you can find them in the passage of scripture below.

Now there are diversities of gifts, but the same Spirit.

And there are differences of administrations, but the same Lord.

And there are diversities of operations, but it is the same God which worketh all in all.

But the manifestation of the Spirit is given to every man to profit withal.

For to one is given by the Spirit the word of wisdom; to another the word of knowledge by the same Spirit;

To another faith by the same Spirit; to another the gifts of healing by the same Spirit;

To another the working of miracles; to another prophecy; to another discerning of spirits; to another divers kinds of tongues; to another the interpretation of tongues:

But all these worketh that one and the selfsame Spirit, dividing to every man severally as he will.

1 Corinthians 12:4-11

Word of Wisdom

This gift is given by the Holy Spirit to enable you to solve complex problems and to take wise decisions. Every complex problem has a solution but unless we are helped by the Holy Spirit through this gift, we often struggle to deal with difficult situations. This gift operated through King Solomon and he was able to solve a complex problem between two women and their babies in the book of 1 Kings chapter 3.

Then came there two women, that were harlots, unto the king, and stood before him.

And the one woman said, O my lord, I and this woman dwell in one house; and I was delivered of a child with her in the house.

And it came to pass the third day after that I was delivered, that this woman was delivered also: and we were together; there was no stranger with us in the house, save we two in the house.

And this woman's child died in the night; because she overlaid it.

And she arose at midnight, and took my son from beside me, while thine handmaid slept, and laid it in her bosom, and laid her dead child in my bosom.

And when I rose in the morning to give my child suck, behold, it was dead: but when I had considered it in the morning, behold, it was not my son, which I did bear.

And the other woman said, Nay; but the living is my son, and the dead is thy son. And this said, No; but the dead is thy son, and the living is my son. Thus they spake before the king.

Then said the king, The one saith, This is my son that liveth, and thy son is the dead: and the other saith, Nay; but thy son is the dead, and my son is the living.

And the king said, Bring me a sword. And they brought a sword before the king.

And the king said, Divide the living child in two, and give half to the one, and half to the other.

Then spake the woman whose the living child was unto the king, for her bowels yearned upon her son, and she said, O my lord, give her the living child, and in no wise

slay it. But the other said, Let it be neither mine nor thine, but divide it.

Then the king answered and said, Give her the living child, and in no wise slay it: she is the mother thereof.

And all Israel heard of the judgment which the king had judged; and they feared the king: for they saw that the wisdom of God was in him, to do judgment.

1 Kings 3:16-28

If the Holy Spirit did not give Solomon this kind of wisdom to judge, he would have been deceived by the woman whose baby was dead.

Word of Knowledge

One day I asked a group of church members to go with me to pray for another church member. However, one of them said she could not come with us. Immediately, the Holy Spirit gave me the word of knowledge that the husband wanted to spend time with her and that is why she gave me that excuse. When I told this church member what the Holy Spirit had allowed me to know, she was baffled and confirmed that it was true. The Holy Spirit enabled me to know a decision that was taken in this church member's bedroom. The word of knowledge is the ability to know things by the help of the Holy Spirit that you could have never known. Sometimes, the Holy Spirit will let you know about someone's past, present and future as He wills. This gift operated through the ministry of Jesus when he was talking to the Samaritan woman at the well.

Jesus saith unto her, Go, call thy husband, and come hither. The woman answered and said, I have no husband.

Jesus said unto her, Thou hast well said, I have no husband:

For thou hast had five husbands; and he whom thou now hast is not thy husband: in that saidst thou truly.

The woman saith unto him, Sir, I perceive that thou art a prophet.

John 4:16-19

Gift of Faith

The gift of faith enables you to believe God for the impossible. This gift is the gift for creating new things and raising the dead. It revives that which is dead and injects life into that which is dead. It is imparted by the Holy Spirit at the moment when it is needed as He the Holy Spirit wills.

Jesus said unto him, If thou canst believe, all things are possible to him that believeth.

Mark 9:23

This gift makes the impossible possible. You can frame your world through this faith by speaking things into existence. By this faith, you can change your circumstances.

Through faith we understand that the worlds were framed by the word of God, so that things which are seen were not made of things which do appear.

Hebrews 11:3

The Gift of Healing

This is the gift that operated throughout the ministry of Jesus and wrought such notable miracles of healings. By this gift, you can lay your hands on the sick and the sick shall be healed.

How God anointed Jesus of Nazareth with the Holy Ghost and with power: who went about doing good, and healing all that were oppressed of the devil; for God was with him.

Acts 10:38

And again, departing from the coasts of Tyre and Sidon, he came unto the sea of Galilee, through the midst of the coasts of Decapolis.

And they bring unto him one that was deaf, and had an impediment in his speech; and they beseech him to put his hand upon him.

And he took him aside from the multitude, and put his fingers into his ears, and he spit, and touched his tongue;

And looking up to heaven, he sighed, and saith unto him, Ephphatha, that is, Be opened.

And straightway his ears were opened, and the string of his tongue was loosed, and he spake plain.

Mark 7:31-35

The Working of Miracles

The Holy Spirit enables believers to wrought special miracles through this gift of the Spirit. This is how the twelve disciples were able to work extraordinary miracles.

And God wrought special miracles by the hands of Paul:

So that from his body were brought unto the sick handkerchiefs or aprons, and the diseases departed from them, and the evil spirits went out of them.

Acts 19:11-12

Gift of Prophecy

Prophecy comes from the Greek word "prophēteia" which means *"prediction."* With this gift, Christians can predict and foretell the future. I have seen this gift operate in my ministry on numerous occasions. We were in church one Sunday and the Holy Spirit allowed me to predict that there was someone in the congregation who will be receiving their indefinite stay that same week. I received a call later that week that the person had received her indefinite stay in the country. This lady came to give her testimony during our Break Every Chain programme.

I told another person who was trying to get a flat to rent, that she was going to get a flat in a specific area directly from a landlord and not through the agency, and it happened exactly as predicted. Prophet Isaiah predicted the birth of Jesus in the Old Testament before it manifested in the New Testament.

Therefore the Lord himself shall give you a sign;

Behold, a virgin shall conceive, and bear a son, and shall call his name Immanuel.

Isaiah 7:14

And she shall bring forth a son, and thou shalt call his name JESUS: for he shall save his people from their sins.

Now all this was done, that it might be fulfilled which was spoken of the Lord by the prophet, saying,

Behold, a virgin shall be with child, and shall bring forth a son, and they shall call his name Emmanuel, which being interpreted is, God with us.

Matthew 1:21-23

As I mentioned earlier on, this gift does not make you a prophet. It does not put you in the office of a prophet so you cannot call yourself a prophet if the Holy Spirit manifests this gift through you as He wills. It also means you cannot just turn the gift on and off, and you cannot decide to predict something about another person's life. The Holy Spirit has to allow you.

Discerning of Spirits

A Christian should be able to tell the difference between the presence of God and the presence of demons.

It is this gift that will enable you to detect the difference. Especially when you are praying for people, you should be able to discern when demons are present. Discerning of spirits simply mean the ability to tell the different kinds of spirits that are present. I have noticed on several occasions when someone falls under the power of God and demons are manifesting through them. Upon discerning, I am able to cast them out by the power of the Holy Spirit.

Beloved, believe not every spirit, but try the spirits whether they are of God: because many false prophets are gone out into the world.

1 John 4:1

The word of God says that we should be able to try spirits. This is not possible without the gift of discerning of spirits. The word "try" in 1 John 4:1, is the Greek word "dokimazō "and it also means *"to discern and to examine."* We as Christians should be able to discern and examine the different spirits in operation in order not be deceived by false prophets.

Diverse Kinds of Tongues

This is a very powerful gift that is given by the Holy Spirit to enable us to speak to the Lord in a heavenly language that no man understands. I have spoken a lot about this gift in chapter 6 so you can refer back to that chapter for more detail.

For he that speaketh in an unknown tongue speaketh not unto men, but unto God: for no man understandeth him; howbeit in the spirit he speaketh mysteries.

1 Corinthians 4:2

Interpretation of Tongues

This gift enables you to understand tongues even though it is a language that no man understands. I have also explained more on this in chapter 6.

To another the working of miracles; to another prophecy; to another discerning of spirits; to another divers kinds of tongues; to another the interpretation of tongues:

1 Corinthians 12:10

Chapter 15

FRUIT OF THE SPIRIT

Unlike the gifts of the Spirit that are imparted to the believer, the fruit of the Spirit develops and forms in a believer as he or she matures in the Lord. It will normally not be found in a baby Christian. Even in the natural life, the more you grow, the wiser you become. A fruit is the part of the tree that is eaten or can be seen by others. Likewise, the fruit of the Spirit is the character and nature of the Holy Spirit that a believer exhibits as he or she grows spiritually. The fruit of the Spirit is also the ability of the believer to walk in the Spirit in order not to fulfil the desires of the flesh.

There are nine fruit of the Spirit in the Bible. However, unlike the gifts of the Spirits which are nine different gifts, the fruit of the Spirit are nine but just one fruit. The word of God does not say "fruits" of the Spirit but "fruit" of the Spirit. This is true because there is only one God and when we become born again Christians we are required to put on the nature, the character and behaviour of God. Since God created us in His own image, we are supposed to be transformed into this image in order to be like Him. It is therefore the fruit of the Spirit that will enable us to become like our maker and to have His divine nature.

Whereby are given unto us exceeding great and precious promises: that by these ye might be partakers of the divine nature, having escaped the corruption that is in the world through lust.

2 Peter 1:4

This means all the nine fruit of the Spirit is required to be formed in a believer. The passage of scripture below lists both the works of the flesh and the fruit of the Spirit. We will focus on the fruit of the Spirit because as this fruit develops in us we will overcome the desires of the flesh.

This I say then, Walk in the Spirit, and ye shall not fulfil the lust of the flesh.

For the flesh lusteth against the Spirit, and the Spirit against the flesh: and these are contrary the one to the other: so that ye cannot do the things that ye would.

But if ye be led of the Spirit, ye are not under the law.

Now the works of the flesh are manifest, which are these; Adultery, fornication, uncleanness, lasciviousness,

Idolatry, witchcraft, hatred, variance, emulations, wrath, strife, seditions, heresies,

Envyings, murders, drunkenness, revellings, and such like: of the which I tell you before, as I have also told you in time past, that they which do such things shall not inherit the kingdom of God.

But the fruit of the Spirit is love, joy, peace, longsuffering, gentleness, goodness, faith,

Meekness, temperance: against such there is no law.

And they that are Christ's have crucified the flesh with the affections and lusts.

If we live in the Spirit, let us also walk in the Spirit.

Galatians 5:16-25

Love

The cardinal sign of Christianity is love and it is a fruit of the Spirit. If a Christian has no love for mankind, no love for God nor the things of God then it is likely that the person is either not saved or has not matured spiritually.

By this shall all men know that ye are my disciples, if ye have love one to another.

John 13:35

The word of God encourages us to love one another because God is love and so is anyone who is born of God. But the one who does not love is not born of God. The word of God stresses that the believer who does not love does not know God.

Beloved, let us love one another: for love is of God; and every one that loveth is born of God, and knoweth God.

1 John 4:7

The fruit of love is important because all the Ten Commandments and all the law and the prophets are summed up in two scriptures that tell us to love God and our neighbour.

Jesus said unto him, Thou shalt love the Lord thy God with all thy heart, and with all thy soul, and with all thy mind.

This is the first and great commandment.

And the second is like unto it, Thou shalt love thy neighbour as thyself.

On these two commandments hang all the law and the prophets.

Matthew 22:37-40

Pray for God to fill you with His love because without the fruit of love, your faith will not work.

For in Jesus Christ neither circumcision availeth any thing, nor uncircumcision; but faith which worketh by love.

Galatians 5:6

Most Christians do not know how to love. They love others because they can get something or they only love those who love them. But the God kind of love or the fruit of love causes you to even love the unlovable. It causes you to love those who have nothing to give back to you and it is not selfish.

Read for yourself the definition of the God kind of love in the scripture passage below. The word "charity" in the scripture is the Greek word "agape" which means *"love."*

Though I speak with the tongues of men and of angels, and have not charity, I am become as sounding brass, or a tinkling cymbal.

And though I have the gift of prophecy, and understand all mysteries, and all knowledge; and though I have all faith, so that I could remove mountains, and have not charity, I am nothing.

And though I bestow all my goods to feed the poor, and though I give my body to be burned, and have not charity, it profiteth me nothing.

Charity suffereth long, and is kind; charity envieth not; charity vaunteth not itself, is not puffed up,

Doth not behave itself unseemly, seeketh not her own, is not easily provoked, thinketh no evil;
Rejoiceth not in iniquity, but rejoiceth in the truth;

Beareth all things, believeth all things, hopeth all things, endureth all things.

Charity never faileth: but whether there be prophecies, they shall fail; whether there be tongues, they shall cease; whether there be knowledge, it shall vanish away.

1 Corinthians 13:1-8

Finally, it is the fruit of love that will cause you to love your enemies.

But I say unto you, Love your enemies, bless them that curse you, do good to them that hate you, and pray for them which despitefully use you, and persecute you;

Matthew 5:44

Joy

It is the fruit of joy that causes a Christian to be happy even when there are issues and difficulties, knowing that God is in control. The joy of the Lord is our strength.

Then he said unto them, Go your way, eat the fat, and drink the sweet, and send portions unto them for whom nothing is prepared: for this day is holy unto our Lord: neither be ye sorry; for the joy of the LORD is your strength.

Nehemiah 8:10

Peace

As a Christian, you must always seek peace because we are the peacemakers of the earth. Some Christians quarrel everywhere and even bring their quarrelsome nature into the church. You see Christians in the same church not talking to each other. This is serious because we are supposed to be peacemakers.

Blessed are the peacemakers: for they shall be called the children of God.

Matthew 5:9

Longsuffering

This is the fruit that will test your patience. Although you do not yet have what you are asking God for, you are able to wait patiently without murmurings or complaints until the Lord grants you your wishes. Some Christians leave churches and turn their backs on God when they feel their prayers have not been answered. It is the fruit of longsuffering that causes a believer to wait patiently in order to inherit the promises of God. The divorce rate in the body of Christ is steadily increasing because of the absence of this fruit of the Spirit in our marriages. No one can take nonsense any more but

I must say that marriage can be full of nonsense. If the fruit of the Spirit called longsuffering is present, these marriages can work out.

That ye be not slothful, but followers of them who through faith and patience inherit the promises.

Hebrews 6:12

Gentleness

This speaks of the demeanour or character of the believer. That is the believer's ability to be kind and good to others.

And be ye kind one to another, tenderhearted, forgiving one another, even as God for Christ's sake hath forgiven you.

Ephesians 4:32

Goodness

As Christians, goodness is a virtue that has to be part of our character. We should naturally aim towards doing good to others.

How God anointed Jesus of Nazareth with the Holy Ghost and with power: who went about doing good,

and healing all that were oppressed of the devil; for God was with him.

Acts 10:38

Faith

This fruit of the spirit speaks of the believer's ability to be totally dependent on God knowing that He will do it. We must have total trust and confidence in God that He is all that we need. With this fruit of the Spirit, we can join with Paul and say that, *"I know whom I have believed."*

For the which cause I also suffer these things: nevertheless I am not ashamed: for I know whom I have believed, and am persuaded that he is able to keep that which I have committed unto him against that day.

2 Timothy 1:12

Meekness

This fruit of the Spirit speaks of humility. A Christian who is humble is a wise Christian and will go very far with the Lord. There are some people in churches who no one can talk to, not even the word of God. These kind of Christians have no boundaries as far as life is concerned because nothing can speak to them. They are so proud that they criticise everything. We must realise that God gives more grace to the humble but He resists the proud.

But he giveth more grace. Wherefore he saith, God resisteth the proud, but giveth grace unto the humble.
James 4:6

You shall be blessed abundantly on this earth if you are humble. Do not say that this is how you are so you cannot change. Allow God to change you so that you can be blessed.

Blessed are the meek: for they shall inherit the earth.
Matthew 5:5

Temperance

This is the ability of the believer to exercise self control. When you become a Christian, you have to restrain yourself from sleeping around like you used to do in the world. You must exercise self control in the area of getting angry so easily and eating when the rest of the church are fasting and praying. Self control is necessary to enable us to deny ourselves in order to follow Christ.

Then said Jesus unto his disciples, If any man will come after me, let him deny himself, and take up his cross, and follow me.

Matthew 16:24

Father in the name of Jesus, help me to mature and exhibit all the fruit of the Spirit. May I not be a baby Christian for the rest of my life, help me to grow in You. In Jesus name, Amen.

Chapter 16

TOKENS AND SYMBOLS OF THE HOLY SPIRIT

There are certain phrases and words used in the Bible which are tokens and symbols of the Holy Spirit. By this I mean the symbols and phrases that represent the Holy Spirit. Each of these symbols are the powerful ways that the Holy Spirit manifests Himself to God's children.

The Breath of God

The breath of God is the symbol of the Holy Spirit as the giver of life. When the breath of God enters into a dead situation, it brings life. It is interesting to know that the breath of the Spirit and the wind of the Spirit are interconnected in that they move together. When Ezekiel was in the valley of dry bones, the Lord commanded him to prophesy to the wind and as he did, breath entered into the dry bones and gave them life. This is very powerful.

I command and prophesy to the wind of the Spirit and I cause the breath of God to enter into every dead situation in your life, in Jesus name.

The hand of the LORD was upon me, and carried me out in the spirit of the LORD, and set me down in the midst of the valley which was full of bones,

And caused me to pass by them round about: and, behold, there were very many in the open valley; and, lo, they were very dry.

And he said unto me, Son of man, can these bones live? And I answered, O Lord GOD, thou knowest.

Again he said unto me, Prophesy upon these bones, and say unto them, O ye dry bones, hear the word of the LORD.

Thus saith the Lord GOD unto these bones; Behold, I will cause breath to enter into you, and ye shall live:

And I will lay sinews upon you, and will bring up flesh upon you, and cover you with skin, and put breath in you, and ye shall live; and ye shall know that I am the LORD.

So I prophesied as I was commanded: and as I prophesied, there was a noise, and behold a shaking, and the bones came together, bone to his bone.

And when I beheld, lo, the sinews and the flesh came up upon them, and the skin covered them above: but there was no breath in them.

Then said he unto me, Prophesy unto the wind, prophesy, son of man, and say to the wind, Thus saith the Lord GOD; Come from the four winds, O breath, and breathe upon these slain, that they may live.

So I prophesied as he commanded me, and the breath came into them, and they lived, and stood up upon their feet, an exceeding great army.

Ezekiel 37:1-10

It was the breath of life that caused Lazarus to come back to life. He was dead for four days and he was stinking, but as the breath of life entered into him, he resurrected.

I see every dead situation in your life coming back to life in Jesus name as the breath of life comes into that situation.

And when he thus had spoken, he cried with a loud voice, Lazarus, come forth.

And he that was dead came forth, bound hand and foot with graveclothes: and his face was bound about with a napkin. Jesus saith unto them, Loose him, and let him go.

John 11:43-44

The Holy Spirit is the same breath that God breathed into man to give man life. God created man out of the dust so man was just clay without blood and without life.

But as soon as God breathed into man, man became a living soul with blood flowing through him and with life.

And the LORD God formed man of the dust of the ground, and breathed into his nostrils the breath of life; and man became a living soul.

Genesis 2:7

The Spirit of God hath made me, and the breath of the Almighty hath given me life.

Job 33:4

It was the same breath that Jesus breathed on the disciples to receive the Holy Spirit.

And when he had said this, he breathed on them, and saith unto them, Receive ye the Holy Ghost:

John 20:22

The Wind of the Spirit

The wind is a powerful force that has the ability to blow and remove mighty trees, uproot strong buildings and destroy a whole nation. These are the negative effects of the natural wind. In the spirit, the Holy Spirit moves as the wind to repair the crooked places of our lives. The wind is able to transform the lives of believers. It was the wind of the Holy Spirit that moved over the earth for the Lord to repair the chaos and confusion on the earth.

And the earth was without form, and void; and darkness was upon the face of the deep. And the Spirit of God moved upon the face of the waters.

Genesis 1:2

The world was dark, void and full of chaos but the Spirit of the Lord moved like a tornado with a mighty force and power to repair this world.

The Holy Spirit is the same wind that moved over the earth to cause the water of destruction to cease when the Lord remembered Noah in the ark.

And God remembered Noah, and every living thing, and all the cattle that was with him in the ark: and God made a wind to pass over the earth, and the waters assuaged;

The fountains also of the deep and the windows of heaven were stopped, and the rain from heaven was restrained;

Genesis 8:1-2

On the day of Pentecost, it was the same wind that descended upon the disciples as a rushing mighty wind and caused them to be filled with the Holy Ghost.

And when the day of Pentecost was fully come, they were all with one accord in one place.

And suddenly there came a sound from heaven as of a rushing mighty wind, and it filled all the house where they were sitting.

Acts 2:1-2

The wind of the Spirit is likened to the born again Christian. Everyone who is born again is also born of the wind.

The wind bloweth where it listeth, and thou hearest the sound thereof, but canst not tell whence it cometh, and whither it goeth: so is every one that is born of the Spirit.

John 3:8

The Holy Spirit as a Dove

When the Holy Spirit comes upon us as a dove, it means the heavens are open over us. It is not good for your heaven to be closed over you. A closed heaven means that God cannot pour out His blessings that are stored in heaven for you. The Holy Spirit is the one who opens the heavens to enable God to pour us out a blessing from where He dwells. Remember while Jesus was being baptised and coming out of the water, the heavens opened and the Spirit of God descended upon Him like a dove.

And Jesus, when he was baptized, went up straightway out of the water: and, lo, the heavens were opened unto him, and he saw the Spirit of God descending like a dove, and lighting upon him:

Matthew 3:16

And the Holy Ghost descended in a bodily shape like a dove upon him, and a voice came from heaven, which said, Thou art my beloved Son; in thee I am well pleased.

Luke 3:22

And John bare record, saying, I saw the Spirit descending from heaven like a dove, and it abode upon him.

And I knew him not: but he that sent me to baptize with water, the same said unto me, Upon whom thou shalt see the Spirit descending, and remaining on him, the same is he which baptizeth with the Holy Ghost.

John 1:32-33

The Holy Spirit as Rain

The rain of the Holy Spirit comes to water the dry places in our lives and causes us to be fruitful and prosperous in every area of our lives. Whether it's your prayer life, reading of the word of God, your education, your work or business or your financial life, the rain of the Holy Spirit is able to make you fruitful. Some Christians are not fruitful both in life and in ministry but as the rain of the Holy Spirit comes upon them, it will cause them to bear fruit both in the house of God and in their personal lives. In the natural, wherever you see rain, the grass looks green and beautiful and there is plenty of food. But where there is drought, there is a lack of beauty and famine arises.

But I see the rain of the Holy Spirit coming upon you right now to cause every drought to cease in your life and cause your life to be beautiful.

It is the rain of the Spirit that causes a believer to blossom and shine. One Sunday morning while in a service, the Lord opened one of my shepherd's eyes and he saw that it was raining all over the room while I was ministering and that the place began to flood. According to this shepherd, he asked the Lord what it meant and the Lord told Him that that it was the Holy Spirit who had come down as rain. Those in the service could also feel the water literally because the place was charged with the presence of the Holy Spirit and there were about eight angels present.

Read the following scriptures.

Until the spirit be poured upon us from on high, and the wilderness be a fruitful field, and the fruitful field be counted for a forest.

Isaiah 32:15

He shall come down like rain upon the mown grass: as showers that water the earth.

Psalm 72:6

Sow to yourselves in righteousness, reap in mercy; break up your fallow ground: for it is time to seek the LORD, till he come and rain righteousness upon you.

Hosea 10:12

Ask ye of the LORD rain in the time of the latter rain; so the LORD shall make bright clouds, and give them showers of rain, to every one grass in the field.

Zechariah 10:1

Then shall we know, if we follow on to know the LORD: his going forth is prepared as the morning; and he shall come unto us as the rain, as the latter and former rain unto the earth.

Hosea 6:3

Be glad then, ye children of Zion, and rejoice in the LORD your God: for he hath given you the former rain moderately, and he will cause to come down for you the rain, the former rain, and the latter rain in the first month.

Joel 2:23

And they waited for me as for the rain; and they opened their mouth wide as for the latter rain.

Job 29:23

He shall come down like rain upon the mown grass: as showers that water the earth.

Psalm 72:6

The Dew of Heaven

The Holy Spirit is likened to the dew of heaven. The dew represents the freshness of the morning. It freshens the green leaves. This means the dew of the Holy Spirit refreshes our Christian lives. We need the dew upon our lives. Isaac blessed Jacob with the dew of heaven. The dew upon our lives signifies the blessings of the Holy Spirit upon our lives. Read the following scriptures.

Therefore God give thee of the dew of heaven, and the fatness of the earth, and plenty of corn and wine:

Genesis 27:28

And Isaac his father answered and said unto him, Behold, thy dwelling shall be the fatness of the earth, and of the dew of heaven from above;

Genesis 27:39

I will be as the dew unto Israel: he shall grow as the lily, and cast forth his roots as Lebanon.

Hosea 14:5

The Holy Spirit as a River

A river flows and overflows. When the Christian is filled with the river of the Holy Spirit it means he or she has been filled until the river is flowing out of them to bless others around them. We must overflow with the Holy Spirit.

In the last day, that great day of the feast, Jesus stood and cried, saying, If any man thirst, let him come unto me, and drink.

He that believeth on me, as the scripture hath said, out of his belly shall flow rivers of living water.

(But this spake he of the Spirit, which they that believe on him should receive: for the Holy Ghost was not yet given; because that Jesus was not yet glorified.)

John 7:37-39

Thou visitest the earth, and waterest it: thou greatly enrichest it with the river of God, which is full of

water: thou preparest them corn, when thou hast so provided for it.

Psalm 65:9

The Holy Spirit as Water or Living Water

The water of the Holy Spirit comes to quench our thirst. In the natural, we drink water when we are thirsty. We drink water to quench our thirst. Many are thirsty and they think that when they get more money it will quench their thirst. But do not be deceived, all the things in this world cannot quench your thirst except the living water of the Holy Spirit.

The woman of Samaria was drawing from a particular well to quench her thirst for many years. But one day, her thirst was quenched when she met Jesus and she was offered to drink the Living Water. Ask the Lord right now to give you the Living Water.

Jesus answered and said unto her, If thou knewest the gift of God, and who it is that saith to thee, Give me to drink; thou wouldest have asked of him, and he would have given thee living water.

John 4:10

But whosoever drinketh of the water that I shall give him shall never thirst; but the water that I shall give

him shall be in him a well of water springing up into everlasting life.

John 4:14

When the poor and needy seek water, and there is none, and their tongue faileth for thirst, I the LORD will hear them, I the God of Israel will not forsake them.

I will open rivers in high places, and fountains in the midst of the valleys: I will make the wilderness a pool of water, and the dry land springs of water.

Isaiah 41:17-18

Read the following scriptures and allow the Living Water of the Holy Spirit to fill you up until you want no more.

In the last day, that great day of the feast, Jesus stood and cried, saying, If any man thirst, let him come unto me, and drink.

He that believeth on me, as the scripture hath said, out of his belly shall flow rivers of living water.

John 7:37-38

For I will pour water upon him that is thirsty, and floods upon the dry ground: I will pour my spirit upon thy seed, and my blessing upon thine offspring:

Isaiah 44:3

Afterward he brought me again unto the door of the house; and, behold, waters issued out from under the threshold of the house eastward: for the forefront of the house stood toward the east, and the waters came down from under from the right side of the house, at the south side of the altar.

Then brought he me out of the way of the gate northward, and led me about the way without unto the utter gate by the way that looketh eastward; and, behold, there ran out waters on the right side.

And when the man that had the line in his hand went forth eastward, he measured a thousand cubits, and he brought me through the waters; the waters were to the ankles.

Again he measured a thousand, and brought me through the waters; the waters were to the knees.
Again he measured a thousand, and brought me through; the waters were to the loins.

Afterward he measured a thousand; and it was a river that I could not pass over: for the waters were risen, waters to swim in, a river that could not be passed over.

And he said unto me, Son of man, hast thou seen this? Then he brought me, and caused me to return to the brink of the river.

Now when I had returned, behold, at the bank of the river were very many trees on the one side and on the other.

Then said he unto me, These waters issue out toward the east country, and go down into the desert, and go into the sea: which being brought forth into the sea, the waters shall be healed.

And it shall come to pass, that every thing that liveth, which moveth, whithersoever the rivers shall come, shall live: and there shall be a very great multitude of fish, because these waters shall come thither: for they shall be healed; and every thing shall live whither the river cometh.

And it shall come to pass, that the fishers shall stand upon it from Engedi even unto Eneglaim; they shall be a place to spread forth nets; their fish shall be according to their kinds, as the fish of the great sea, exceeding many.

But the miry places thereof and the marishes thereof shall not be healed; they shall be given to salt.

And by the river upon the bank thereof, on this side and on that side, shall grow all trees for meat, whose leaf shall not fade, neither shall the fruit thereof be consumed: it shall bring forth new fruit according to his months, because their waters they issued out of the sanctuary: and the fruit thereof shall be for meat, and the leaf thereof for medicine.

Ezekiel 47:1-12

And it shall come to pass in the last days, saith God, I will pour out of my Spirit upon all flesh: and your sons and your daughters shall prophesy, and your young men shall see visions, and your old men shall dream dreams:

Acts 2:17

The Holy Spirit as a Cloud

The Holy Spirit as the cloud represents the presence of the Lord. Wherever the cloud was, the Lord was there and His presence fills that place. It is this cloud that fills a church when people are worshiping and praising the Lord.

I was a praise and worship leader on the university campus. While leading praise and worship one Sunday morning, the presence of God filled the church so much that you could tangibly feel the thickness of the glory of God in the room. When the pastor took the microphone to preach, he proclaimed that the presence of the Lord was there indeed. This is exactly what happened in the book of 2 Chronicles.

It came even to pass, as the trumpeters and singers were as one, to make one sound to be heard in praising and thanking the LORD; and when they lifted up their voice with the trumpets and cymbals and instruments of musick, and praised the LORD, saying, For he is good; for his mercy endureth for ever: that then the house was filled with a cloud, even the house of the LORD;

So that the priests could not stand to minister by reason of the cloud: for the glory of the LORD had filled the house of God.

2 Chronicles 5:13-14

Another important thing about the cloud is that the Lord always speaks through the cloud or His presence. Listen carefully when the presence of God is available because He speaks.

While he yet spake, behold, a bright cloud overshadowed them: and behold a voice out of the cloud, which said,

This is my beloved Son, in whom I am well pleased; hear ye him.

Matthew 17:5

Read the following scriptures.

And it came to pass, when the priests were come out of the holy place, that the cloud filled the house of the LORD,

So that the priests could not stand to minister because of the cloud: for the glory of the LORD had filled the house of the LORD.

1 Kings 8:10-11

And the LORD went before them by day in a pillar of a cloud, to lead them the way; and by night in a pillar of fire, to give them light; to go by day and night:

Exodus 13:21

And it came to pass, as Aaron spake unto the whole congregation of the children of Israel, that they looked toward the wilderness, and, behold, the glory of the LORD appeared in the cloud.

Exodus 16:10

And the LORD said unto Moses, Lo, I come unto thee in a thick cloud, that the people may hear when I speak with thee, and believe thee for ever. And Moses told the words of the people unto the LORD.

Exodus 19:9

And it came to pass on the third day in the morning, that there were thunders and lightnings, and a thick cloud upon the mount, and the voice of the trumpet exceeding loud; so that all the people that was in the camp trembled.

Exodus 19:16

And Moses went up into the mount, and a cloud covered the mount.

And the glory of the LORD abode upon mount Sinai, and the cloud covered it six days: and the seventh day he called unto Moses out of the midst of the cloud.

And the sight of the glory of the LORD was like devouring fire on the top of the mount in the eyes of the children of Israel.

And Moses went into the midst of the cloud, and gat him up into the mount: and Moses was in the mount forty days and forty nights.

Exodus 24:15-18

And the LORD descended in the cloud, and stood with

him there, and proclaimed the name of the LORD.

Exodus 34:5

And on the day that the tabernacle was reared up the cloud covered the tabernacle, namely, the tent of the testimony: and at even there was upon the tabernacle as it were the appearance of fire, until the morning.

So it was alway: the cloud covered it by day, and the appearance of fire by night.

And when the cloud was taken up from the tabernacle, then after that the children of Israel journeyed: and in the place where the cloud abode, there the children of Israel pitched their tents.

At the commandment of the LORD the children of Israel journeyed, and at the commandment of the LORD they pitched: as long as the cloud abode upon the tabernacle they rested in their tents.

And when the cloud tarried long upon the tabernacle many days, then the children of Israel kept the charge of the LORD, and journeyed not.

And so it was, when the cloud was a few days upon the tabernacle; according to the commandment of the

LORD they abode in their tents, and according to the commandment of the LORD they journeyed.

And so it was, when the cloud abode from even unto the morning, and that the cloud was taken up in the morning, then they journeyed: whether it was by day or by night that the cloud was taken up, they journeyed.

Or whether it were two days, or a month, or a year, that the cloud tarried upon the tabernacle, remaining thereon, the children of Israel abode in their tents, and journeyed not: but when it was taken up, they journeyed.

Numbers 9:15-22

And when he had spoken these things, while they beheld, he was taken up; and a cloud received him out of their sight.

Acts 1:9

The Holy Spirit as Fire

Have you heard the saying that there is no smoke without fire? This is because wherever there is smoke, it means there is a source of fire. Now the cloud of the Holy Spirit is like a smoke and as a result the source is fire. So when you read through the Bible, wherever you see the cloud, you also see the fire. The Holy Spirit is the fire that burns in the Christian's life and sets them ablaze for Jesus. The fire burns the chaffs from our lives, the fire keeps us holy and righteous and the fire makes us sharp. Fire gives us energy and enables the believer to walk as a Christian.

And it shall come to pass, that he that is left in Zion, and he that remaineth in Jerusalem, shall be called holy, even every one that is written among the living in Jerusalem:

When the Lord shall have washed away the filth of the daughters of Zion, and shall have purged the blood of Jerusalem from the midst thereof by the spirit of judgment, and by the spirit of burning.

Isaiah 4:3-4

Read the scriptures below.

And the LORD went before them by day in a pillar of a cloud, to lead them the way; and by night in a pillar of fire, to give them light; to go by day and night:

Exodus 13:21

And the sight of the glory of the LORD was like devouring fire on the top of the mount in the eyes of the children of Israel.

Exodus 24:17

For the cloud of the LORD was upon the tabernacle by day, and fire was on it by night, in the sight of all the house of Israel, throughout all their journeys.

Exodus 40:38

And on the day that the tabernacle was reared up the cloud covered the tabernacle, namely, the tent of the testimony: and at even there was upon the tabernacle as it were the appearance of fire, until the morning.

Numbers 9:15

Then the fire of the LORD fell, and consumed the burnt sacrifice, and the wood, and the stones, and the dust, and licked up the water that was in the trench.

1 Kings 18:38

And the LORD will create upon every dwelling place of mount Zion, and upon her assemblies, a cloud and smoke by day, and the shining of a flaming fire by night: for upon all the glory shall be a defence.

Isaiah 4:5

For the LORD thy God is a consuming fire, even a jealous God.

Deuteronomy 4:24

Understand therefore this day, that the LORD thy God is he which goeth over before thee; as a

consuming fire he shall destroy them, and he shall bring them down before thy face: so shalt thou drive them out, and destroy them quickly, as the LORD hath said unto thee.

Deuteronomy 9:3

And there appeared unto them cloven tongues like as of fire, and it sat upon each of them.

Acts 2:3

For our God is a consuming fire.

Hebrews 12:29

The Holy Spirit as the Finger of God

The Holy Spirit as the finger of God comes to demonstrate God's power by causing signs and wonders to happen. The finger of God comes to rebuke and cast out demons as well as change situations and circumstances. Jesus casted out devils by the finger of God. Moses performed various signs and wonders by the finger of God.

But if I with the finger of God cast out devils, no doubt the kingdom of God is come upon you.

Luke 11:20

Then the magicians said unto Pharaoh, This is the finger of God: and Pharaoh's heart was hardened, and he hearkened not unto them; as the LORD had said.

Exodus 8:19

The Ten Commandments were written with the finger of God. The Holy Spirit was the pen the Lord used to write the Ten Commandments.

And he gave unto Moses, when he had made an end of communing with him upon mount Sinai,
two tables of testimony, tables of stone, written with the finger of God.

Exodus 31:18

And the LORD delivered unto me two tables of stone written with the finger of God; and on them was written according to all the words, which the LORD spake with you in the mount out of the midst of the fire in the day of the assembly.

Deuteronomy 9:10

The Holy Spirit as the Hand of the Lord

The Hand of the Lord comes upon us to empower us to do exploits for the Lord. It was the hand of the Lord that came upon Elijah to run faster than Ahab although Ahab was sitting on a chariot. When the hand of the Lord comes upon you, you can run faster than your enemies.

You will catch up and overtake all those who think they have gone ahead of you and look down upon you.

I see God lifting you up as His mighty hand comes upon you.

And the hand of the LORD was on Elijah; and he girded up his loins, and ran before Ahab to the entrance of Jezreel.

1 Kings 18:46

The hand of the LORD was upon me, and carried me out in the spirit of the LORD, and set me down in the midst of the valley which was full of bones,

Ezekiel 37:1

And all they that heard them laid them up in their hearts, saying, What manner of child shall this be! And the hand of the Lord was with him.

Luke 1:66

The Holy Spirit as Wine

Wine is a symbol of the Holy Spirit in that when a person is influenced by the Holy Spirit they sometimes behave as a drunk person. In Ephesians 5:18, the word of God entreats us to be filled with the wine of the Holy Spirit instead of the wine of the world which is alcohol.

And be not drunk with wine, wherein is excess; but be filled with the Spirit;

Ephesians 5:18

When John the Baptist was born, the Lord instructed his parents not to give the child the wine of the world because He was going to be filled with the Holy Spirit or the Wine of the Spirit. This point is explained further in chapter 12, under drunkenness as a physical manifestation of the Holy Spirit.

For he shall be great in the sight of the Lord, and shall drink neither wine nor strong drink; and he shall be filled with the Holy Ghost, even from his mother's womb.

Luke 1:15

Oil as a Symbol of the Holy Spirit

Throughout the Bible, oil has been used as a symbol of the Holy Spirit to anoint, consecrate and separate Christians to God to do His work. For instance, the Lord instructed the prophet Samuel to anoint Saul as a King over Israel. Note that Samuel took a vial of oil and anointed Saul. As soon as the oil of the Spirit came upon Saul, he was turned into another man and he began to prophesy. Remember that oil is not the Holy Spirit but it is just a symbol representing Him.

Then Samuel took a vial of oil, and poured it upon his head, and kissed him, and said, Is it not because the LORD hath anointed thee to be captain over his inheritance?

1 Samuel 10:1

I see the oil of the Spirit coming upon your life and transforming you into a great and mighty man and woman of God. People will begin to ask whether you are also among the great men and women of God.

And it came to pass, when all that knew him beforetime saw that, behold, he prophesied among the prophets, then the people said one to another, What is this that is come unto the son of Kish? Is Saul also among the prophets?

1 Samuel 10:11

One day, while in a service, I felt oil dripping on my face. I touched my face to feel the oil but it was not a physical oil. The Lord was anointing me with the oil of the Spirit. He was setting me apart to do His work. Many of us know the oil in the natural realm but I want you to yearn for the oil of the Spirit. It is because it already exists in the Spirit that is why it is represented physically. It is this same oil of the Spirit that the prophet Samuel used to anoint King David.

The word of God states that as soon as David was anointed with the oil, the Spirit of the Lord came upon Him.

Then Samuel took the horn of oil, and anointed him in the midst of his brethren: and the Spirit of the LORD came upon David from that day forward. So Samuel rose up, and went to Ramah.

1 Samuel 16:13

The Holy Spirit as the Glory of God

The glory of the Lord is that which makes us beautiful and causes us to shine. Sometimes you see a pastor preaching and he begins to glow on stage. It the Holy Spirit as the glory of God that causes that pastor to glow.

It does not matter how ugly your situation is, God will make you beautiful. It does not matter how dirty your life has been, God will make you beautiful. I see you shining in Jesus name.

Then a cloud covered the tent of the congregation, and the glory of the LORD filled the tabernacle.

And Moses was not able to enter into the tent of the congregation, because the cloud abode thereon, and the glory of the LORD filled the tabernacle.

And when the cloud was taken up from over the tabernacle, the children of Israel went onward in all their journeys:

But if the cloud were not taken up, then they journeyed not till the day that it was taken up.

For the cloud of the LORD was upon the tabernacle by day, and fire was on it by night, in the sight of all the house of Israel, throughout all their journeys.

Exodus 40:34-38

PRAYER OF SALVATION

After reading this book, you may want to know and experience this blessed Holy Spirit. You can, right now. The first step to receiving the Holy Spirit is to be born again. If you want to accept Jesus Christ as your Lord and Saviour today, please say this prayer.

My Father in heaven, I recognise that I am a sinner.
I recognise that the Lord Jesus died for me and paid the penalty of my sins.

Dear Lord, today I repent of my sins and I accept Jesus Christ as my Lord and my Saviour.
Wash me with your blood and make me holy.

Please write my name in the book of life and give me the grace to serve you for the rest of my life.
Thank you that I am born again.
Amen.

Other Books by Rev. Ernest Addo

Three Dimensions of Man

The Foundations of True Faith

The Father's Love

How to Pray: 60 Minutes In His Presence

Spiritual Emergency

To order copies or for more information,
please contact ernest.addo1@yahoo.com.